Contemporary Chord KHANCEPTS

PUBLISHED BY
MANHATTAN MUSIC, INC.™
©1996 MANHATTAN MUSIC, INC.™

BY STEVE KHAN

D1737389

MANHATTAN Music PUBLICATIONS™

Alfred

Table of Contents

Audio Tracks

TRACK	DESCRIPTION/TITLE
[1]	Tuning Notes (A = 440)
[2]	E♭ major Triad Piece (Example 5)
[3]	E♭ major Triad Piece (without guitar)
[4]	G Shuffle Blues (Examples 7–10 and 12–13)
[5]	G Shuffle Blues (without guitar)
[6]	G Gospel Blues (Examples 18–19) For play-along, use track [5]
[7]	Blues/Rock Shuffle (use with any G blues)
[8]	G Blues/Latin (use with any G blues)
[9]	G Minor Blues (Example 11)
[10]	G Minor Blues (without guitar)
[11]	F Jazz Blues (Examples 14–15)
[12]	F Jazz Blues (without guitar)
[13]	Harmony Across the Strings (B♭maj) (Example 20–31)
[14]	ii–V–I–VI7 (B♭maj) (without guitar)
[15]	ii–V–I–VI7 over G Pedal (even 8th-notes) (Examples 32–36)
[16]	G Pedal (even 8th-notes) (without guitar)
[17]	Chord Exercise in Sequence over C Pedal (Examples 41–44)
[18]	C Pedal (even 8th-notes) (without guitar)
[19]	Style—3/4 Latin Vamp in G (Examples 45–47)
[20]	3/4 Latin Vamp in G (without guitar)
[21]	ii–V–I Cadences (B♭maj) (Examples 52A–D)
[22]	ii–V–I (B♭maj) (without guitar)
[23]	ii∅–V–i Cadences (Gm) (Examples 53A–D)
[24]	ii∅–V–i (Gm) (without guitar)
[25]	Major/minor Exercise in G (Example 58–62) For play-along, use track [16]
[26]	G Pedal/Latin
[27]	"Mundo Desmondo" (Examples 63–65)
[28]	"Mundo Desmondo" (without guitar)
[29]	"Some Things You're Not" (Examples 66A–C)
[30]	"Some Things You're Not" (without guitar)
[31]	Gm7–E♭maj7♯4 Exercise (examples 67–69)
[32]	Gm7–E♭maj7♯4 Exercise (without guitar)
[33]	"Don Grolnelius" (Unit 19—improvised piece)
[34]	C Pedal Shuffle (without guitar)
[35]	"Cintura City" (A♭7–B♭m7 Latin Vamp)
[36]	A♭7–B♭m7 Latin Vamp (without guitar)
[37]	"Sliceville" (B♭ Latin Blues)
[38]	B♭ Latin Blues (without guitar)
[39]	"Khalatmo" (F7–B♭7–B♭7–F7 Latin Vamp)
[40]	F7–B♭7–B♭7–F7 Latin Vamp (without guitar)
[41]	"Gracinha" (ii–V–I–VI7 B♭maj Latin Vamp)
[42]	ii–V–I–VI7 B♭maj Latin Vamp (without guitar)

Special Thanks

My very Special Thanks to the following people:

Al Gorgoni . . . for your friendship, generosity, talents, and tireless efforts in helping me assemble the play-along sequences which grace these CDs and which have been a part of my clinics and private teaching for the past several years. I'm so grateful and could NOT have done this without you, or your family. And to: Rob Wallis, Aaron Stang, Tom Roed, Bob Sherwin, Mike Selverne, Fruko, Christine Martin, Malcolm and Nina Pollack, Rob Mounsey, Felicia Michael, Oscar Hernandez, Manolo Badrena, Marc Quiñones, Blanca Lopez, Clifford Carter, National Guitar Summer Workshop, Ned Shaw, David Tan, Mike Landy, Colin Schofield, Yuny Reyes, Ed Rak, Dan Seeff, Bill and Kristin Hart, Stan Smith, John Harris, Dan Keller, Anthony Jackson, Ruben Rodriguez, Patrizio Chiozza, Kenny Inaoka, Sabina and Seth Ornstein, Oscar D'Leon, Sergio George, Robin Gould, Freddy Zerbib, Adam Gorgoni, Julian Gorgoni, Bayamo, Bernie Minoso, Bernie Williams, Derek Jeter, Puerto Rico All-Stars, Dennis Chambers, Ellen and Barry Birnbaum, The Shapiros, Donn Cunningham, Ron Carter, Juan Luis Guerra, Astellia Diaz, Clare Fischer, Poncho Sanchez, Doug West, Betty Demont-Rahjou, Jimmy Anton, Jean-Michel Folon, Esther Flores, and John Locke.

Acknowledgments

Gibson Guitars (Jimmy Archey), Dean Markley Strings (Rich Friedrich), Sadowsky Guitars (Roger Sadowsky and Ken Fallon), Walter Woods Amps (Walter Woods), custom Audio Electronics (Bob Bradshaw), Aguilar Electronics (Alex Aguilar), Korg/Marshall (Mitch Colby), Yamaha (Masaaki Naito), Ibanez (John Lomas), Danny K. Music Services, The Latin Quarter (Carla Reyes), and Manny's (The Godldrich Family) Soundsmith (Harry Kolbe & Eric Bradley).

Dedication

The work in this book is dedicated with love and gratitude to my mother, Gloria and to my sister, Laurie . . . and, as always, to my dear son, Heath.

Correspondence

Please feel free to visit my website: **http://www.stevekhan.com** and, if you like, write to me anytime via the **CONTACT STEVE** page at the site.

Credits

Editors: Robert Wallis and Aaron Stang
Music Engraving and Book Layout/Design: Chelsea Music Engraving
Cover Design: Hélène Côtè
Back Cover Illustration: Ned Shaw
Recording Information:

Produced by:	Steve Khan
Associate Producers:	Al Gorgoni and Malcolm Pollack
Executive Producers:	Rob Wallis
Programmed and Sequenced by:	Steve Khan, Al Gorgoni, and Adam Gorgoni
Recorded at:	Lightstream Studios, October 4, and 7, 1996
Recorded and Mixed by:	Malcolm Pollack
Additional Sequencing:	Rob Mounsey
Sequenced at:	Flying Monkey Studios
Flying Monkey Assistant:	Felicia Michael
Post-Production:	The Review Room
Engineer:	Mike Landy

Introduction

It seems strange that with our instrument, in the world of pop and rock music, there could exist such a thing as a "rhythm guitar" player. A guitarist who just plays the chords. And, a "lead guitar" player, one who only plays solos, fills, and licks. I find this odd because I believe that you must try to play ALL of the instrument as best you can. Obviously, you'll have strong and weak points, but don't let your shortcomings get the best of you. You CAN develop into a well-rounded musician and guitarist.

Since the '80s, music education has advanced faster than one can keep up with. During the '60s, when I was trying to learn how to play the guitar, you had private teachers, a few books, and exchanges of information with friends, but mainly YOU HAD YOUR EARS! If you couldn't hear things quickly, you were lost. No play along CDs, no videos, instructional books with cassettes, no "REAL BOOK," and no Jamey Aebersold's "JAZZ AIDS" service.

As a teacher I've been amazed at the technical advances on the instrument. Never has there been so many players with such incredible technique. Often-times that ability has come at the expense of a comprehensive knowledge of music: harmony and theory. In my experience, that has translated into students allowing their chordal knowledge to lag far, far behind. So, as a teacher, I've tried to bring in the extremes and share my concepts about being able to put to use all the possibilities the guitar offers for more complete expression.

After I had moved to New York City in January of 1970, I began to slowly add more guitar and music books to my library. I recall purchasing several "Chord Dictionary" publications, some with as many as 80,000 chords. I remember thinking, "How could there possibly be THAT many chords?" As I studied these books and continued to learn about the guitar, I realized that most of these chords just fulfilled a number in the book but proved to be virtually useless when making music with other musicians. In this book, I've tried my best to make certain that everything presented has the potential to be used in a variety of settings. I would be the first to admit that I have not covered every single possibility, but, the work assembled here will certainly serve as an excellent source to which to refer anytime.

In a sense, for my own approach, I've tried to view things in a more pianistic manner. The pianist can accompany their right-hand lines with their left-hand. So, in part, I've worked at playing the guitar with this kind of approach in mind, but, the key difference for me is NEVER view the left-hand aspect as "just a bunch of chords!" The concept is to ALWAYS hear the top note of any chord as having melodic content. This is of crucial importance. Your lines and your chords are of equal import and can function beautifully together in your hands.

My method for sharing this concept is actually a complete contradiction to the end result we hope to achieve. By that I mean, I treat chords as totally separate from the linear work. At the start, the two are only joined by harmonic theory. And, as the work progresses, the lines and chords slowly begin to function together. As there are many excellent books and videos which concentrate on the linear side of the instrument and improvising, I have chosen to focus on a chordal approach which can join those lines.

It's my sincere hope that you will work slowly through this method from the building blocks to the more sophisticated concepts. Approach things in small study units by making a series of short term goals for yourself — something you CAN accomplish in a reasonable amount of time. You might find it difficult to place a specific time frame for the mastery of these concepts, but patience and a steady course will surely win out in the end.

All the best,

New York City, November 1996

Steve Khan admits that, when he was a teenager, "I was a terrible drummer with no musical training. I had developed a love for the guitar and, when I was 19, switched instruments. I was determined that I would not make the same mistakes I had made with the drums, and studied composition and theory at UCLA, along with private guitar lessons from Ron Anthony." In 1970 he moved to New York City.

From this point forward, so much of Steve's career is well documented. In 1974, he performed in one of the first contemporary jazz guitar duos with Larry Coryell. During this same period, he became a member of the Brecker Brothers Band. His first recordings as a leader were a trio of albums for Columbia Records titled: "Tightrope" (1977), "The Blue Man" (1978) and "Arrows" (1979). These recordings featured Randy and Michael Brecker, David Sanborn, Don Grolnick, Mike Mainieri, Will Lee, Steve Gadd, and others. In 1994, Sony Music/Columbia released a CD compilation drawn from these three LPs titled, "The Collection."

In 1980, Steve recorded a brilliant solo acoustic guitar album, "Evidence," which paid tribute to his earliest jazz inspirations and served to establish him as one of the great interpreters of the music of Thelonious Monk. Between 1981 and 1985, he worked and recorded with his quartet, Eyewitness, which included Anthony Jackson, Manolo Badrena, and Steve Jordan. Together they made three recordings: "Eyewitness" (1981), "Modern Times"/"Blades" (1982) and "Casa Loco" (1983). Steve joined Joe Zawinul's Weather Update for it's one and only tour in 1986. This was followed by an innovative duet recording with keyboardist Rob Mounsey. The Grammy-nominated CD was titled "Local Color," and was released in 1987. 1989 saw the resurrection of Eyewitness with Dave Weckl replacing Steve Jordan for the "Public Access" CD. Since that time, Steve has added two straight ahead jazz recordings which featured Ron Carter and Al Foster. "Let's Call This" and "Headline" were released in 1991 and 1992 respectively. In 1994, Steve found himself back in the company of Anthony Jackson and Manolo Badrena, adding Dennis Chambers and Michael Brecker for "Crossings," which was dedicated to the memory of his late father, lyricist Sammy Cahn.

Recently, Steve has contributed to several special projects. His unique medley of two George Harrison tunes graced Mike Mainieri's NYC Records "Come Together — A Guitar Tribute to The Beatles." Here he was accompanied by Marc Johnson, Peter Erskine and Nana Vasconcelos. Special Olympics and the Holiday Season brought Steve together again with the Brecker Brothers for a Salsa-styled interpretation of his father's one true Christmas song, "The Christmas Waltz," which appeared on Blue Note's "Jazz to the World" CD. In 1996, Steve teamed with Argentine vocalist Gabriela Anders, Rob Mounsey and New York Salsa All-Stars: Ruben Rodriguez, Marc Quiñones and Papo Pepin to contribute "Don't Worry Baby" ("No Te Preocupes Nena") to "Wouldn't It Be Nice," a tribute to Brian Wilson.

Recorded in September of 1996, "Got My Mental" brings Steve together for the first time with John Patitucci and Jack DeJohnette. The CD again finds him using his unique playing and arranging perspective to interpret the works of Wayne Shorter, Ornette Coleman, Lee Morgan, and Eddie Harris; as well as standards by Rodgers and Hammerstein, and Sammy Cahn and James Van Heusen.

Throughout his long and distinguished career, Steve has recorded with such diverse artists as Miles Davis, Steely Dan, James Brown, Aretha Franklin, Quincy Jones, Eddie Palmieri, Freddie Hubbard, Steps Ahead, and others too numerous to list. He has also produced recordings for fellow guitarists Larry Coryell, Mike Stern, Bireli Lagrene and Bill Connors as well as pianist Eliane Elias. In addition to this book, he has published three other highly regarded books: "The Wes Montgomery Guitar Folio," "Pat Martino: The Early Years," and "Guitar Workshop Series — Steve Khan" (which really functions as an Eyewitness Songbook). In addition to recording and performing, Steve is an active clinician and teacher.

range of the guitar

To the eyes and ears of many, the range of the guitar, at its outer reaches, can at times seem like it rivals the piccolo. If the following diagram is studied carefully, the truth about where our instrument really functions can become clear. If we're to be honest with ourselves then we will readily admit that, in our lower register, we're operating in the territory of most bass instruments; and, in our middle to upper registers, we're essentially operating in the center of most keyboards. Whether we're the principal melodic instrument (the soloist) or simply part of a basic 4-piece rhythm section (keyboard(s)/guitar/bass/drums), it's essential to gain an understanding of how our instrument best functions.

Throughout recent decades there have been a multitude of chord books offering thousands upon thousands of chord shapes for the guitar. It is my experience that in the context of making music with other instruments, most of the chord voicings which employ the "E" and "A" strings are essentially useless. The reason being, that when we're using these two strings, we're likely to be in the way of the bass, and potentially clouding the lower register of the keyboard. If one examines the style of Wes Montgomery, it's obvious that he used full sounding voicings as an active part of his style and sounded tremendous. BUT, he was the LEADER, and the arrangements were built around what he was playing. Pianists and organists knew, or learned, how to stay out of the way. In many rock, heavy metal, country, and folk musics, it's stylistically important for the guitar to use the lower strings. In the long run, always try to do what's right for the music as a whole!

As this book unfolds, I hope to make a strong case for using 2, 3, and 4-note voicings which lay across your D–G–B–E strings. As you work at developing an evolved sense of harmony and theory, I believe that you'll find this concept extremely useful in, firstly, just playing with a bassist, and later with the addition of a keyboard. I have tried to supply you with as many options as possible. When you put these concepts to use, it then becomes a matter of your own sense of harmony and taste.

Written   **Sounds**

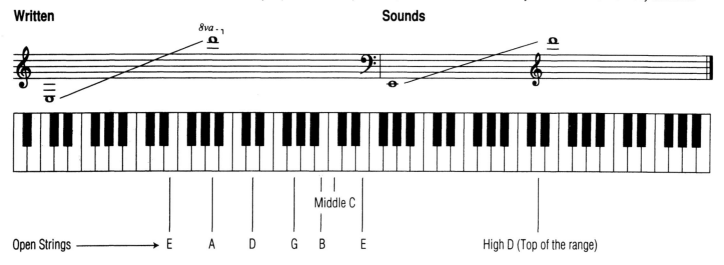

Open Strings ——————→ E   A   D   G   B   E   High D (Top of the range)

Middle C

fingerings

As I worked at amending my personal approach, which was fundamentally for groups without a keyboard player, I gradually began to adjust all my fingerings. This became especially true for the 2- and 3-note chord formations. These forms, when played as part of a voicing employing a bass note on the "E" or "A" strings would be fingered in the traditional manner. I chose to finger these voicings in an individual way, not as if I had simply lifted off the finger which would have been playing the bass note. My reasoning in doing this was to try and smooth out — make as legato as possible — the flow from one voicing into another. I feel confident, that if given the time to sink in, usage of my fingerings will give you great results, especially if you're not happy with the current state of your chordal movements.

pick
pick and fingers
fingers

No matter how proficient you become in playing with a pick, as your abilities with chords broaden there will be times when the use of either the "pick and claw" technique or fingers alone will prove more expressive. The advantage of these techniques is the ability to bring out the top voice of any chord and insure that it speaks clearly as a melodic voice.

By using a pick only, no matter how quickly you strike across a chord, the higher voices will always be milliseconds late. By using the pick plus two or three fingers or fingers only, you can pluck all the strings simultaneously and, perhaps best of all, bring out the top voice a little more.

So, if you're playing lines with a pick and some chords with fingers only, how does one solve this back and forth problem? Several years ago, at a clinic, someone asked, "While you were playing, I noticed every so often your pick would disappear when you played chords, where did it go?" At that moment, I honestly did not know what he was talking about. At first I asked if I'd put the pick between my teeth. He said, "No." So, I tried to recreate the circumstances and, after a while, I realized that I would slip the pick between the 1st and 2nd fingers of my right hand in the area between the 2nd knuckle and where the finger joins the hand. So, when playing a 4-note chord, the thumb strikes the "D" string, 1st finger the "G" string, 2nd finger the "B" string, and the 3rd finger is free to bring out the top voice on the "E" string by applying a little more force. It will take a lot of consistent practice, but you CAN do it!

superimposition of the iim7 on V7 chords

It seems so simple that a keyboard player would look at a chord voicing played across two hands and see it as, for example, some form of G7 chord. Often on guitar, we can play only a portion of the chord voicing. For example: We might play only what the right-hand of the keyboard is playing—a part of that G7 chord. We might view our voicing as perhaps a Dm7 over the bassist's "G," or any number of other options. In discussions here, and with one another, it's fine to look at things in this rather separated manner. Just don't lose sight of what the larger harmonic picture really is.

In this book we will build your chordal vocabulary from:

a) a 2-note (guide tones) approach,

b) through traditional and extended 3-note voicings,

c) and finally to 4-note chords all built upon upper extensions of basic chord.

Throughout the book, I'll be referring to iim7 and V7 chords as being related and interchangeable. If you build chord voicings up from the 5th degree of G7 (D) you would construct Dm, Dm7, Dm9, etc. In so doing, you would be extending the harmony of G7 by adding the 9th (A), the 11th (C), and the 13th (E): G7: G B D F

Chord Tones: 1 3 5 ♭7 9 11 13

Dm9: D F A C E

Chord Tones: 1 ♭3 5 ♭7 9

Example 1: G7 Chord Tones

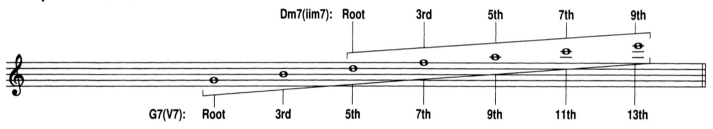

If we improvise using D minor voicings we'd constantly create these extensions of G7 and probably produce, what I would attempt to describe as a very majestic feeling in the music.

If we see all this activity as functioning in the key of C major, then "G" is the V7 (dominant 7th) and "D" is the iim7. In order to produce this "majestic" harmonic effect you're always superimposing iim7 chord voicings over the root of the V7.

Example 2: Harmonized Major Scale

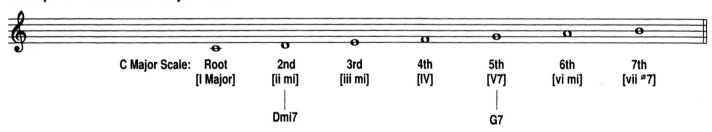

As my own concept has evolved, I find that I rarely play a guitar voicing utilizing my low "A" or "E" strings. I've found that this keeps me out of the bass player's way, and, seems to free us both. More importantly, it expands our improvisational boundaries. This book will not deal with the traditional guitar chords which utilize voicings where the lowest note is on the "A" or "E" strings. If you feel the need to shore-up this part of your knowledge, there are many excellent publications which treat this area in detail. To name a few of the authors: Mickey Baker, Joe Pass, and Ted Greene. As we expand on this concept and introduce progressively more and more ambiguous 3- and 4-note voicings, you'll find that the bass part and the music grow freer and freer because the possibilities for spontaneous reharmonization of any chord become endless. And, you and your music will benefit most!

triads

After some 20 years of teaching, it still amazes me that so many exceptionally gifted guitarists could develop great technical facility in the linear aspects of the instrument and totally ignore the most basic chordal components. I'm speaking of the fundamental 2-note intervallic relationships and the simple, but essential, major and minor triads. Though this book deals with the advanced uses of harmony, I feel that it's important that the usages of triads be included.

Not too long ago in an interview, Robben Ford stated how he is always asked about his soloing. He tries to impress upon younger players that, except for a few moments of soloing, the guitarist must function as an accompanist most of the time. I couldn't agree more with this assessment. So we must acknowledge that often we will be asked to function as a small part in the greater context of someone else's music. As a supporting player, we must operate in a sonic place that leaves room for the keyboards and bass to move freely. Obviously, if a piece of music is built around the guitar, the other instruments must then allow us the same latitude. This means that most times we will play 2-, 3-, and 4-note chords with the highest voice usually on the "B" or "E" strings. This is where a thorough knowledge of the basic triads becomes so useful.

It's been my experience that using triads in an accompaniment figure is most useful in R&B, Funk, and Jazz-Rock Fusion where the underpinning is essentially based upon the two former styles. The guitar is generally called upon for its percussive qualities and it is for this reason that I've only presented triads where the highest note is on the "B" or "E" strings. I've chosen to omit triads with the top voice on the "D" or "G" strings because I find these voicings sound much to dark to cut through most textures. It is important to know them, but, I'm going to leave that pursuit up to you.

Example 3: G Triads

Top voice on "E" String

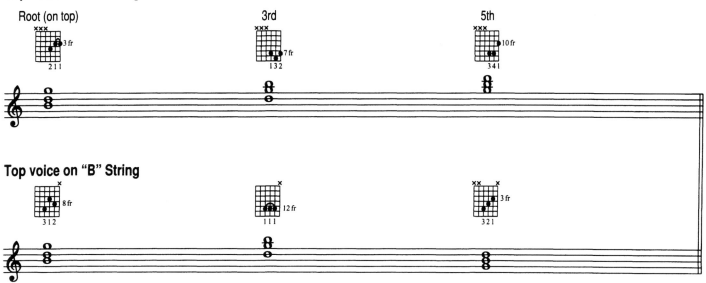

Top voice on "B" String

Example 3A: G Minor Triads

Top voice on "E" String

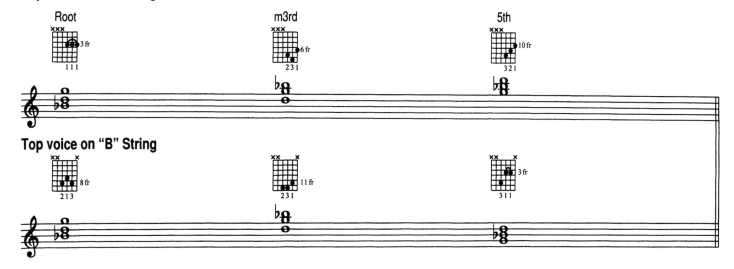

Top voice on "B" String

triad superimposition

The following "Triad Superimposition" chart is an important one; once you understand its usage you can continually refer back to it. What I've done is to take a single bass note, the root in most cases, and used triads (both major and minor) which ascend chromatically over the root. As you're provided with a long "G" pedal vamp on the recording this work is presented over "G." I've analyzed the "real chord" function (its theoretically correct name) and the mode or scale one might need to know for improvising. When all is said and done, you'll actually have to know this information for the eleven other roots.

Let's look at the first example: F/G (an F triad over a G bass note). Although this chord can serve several functions, it's usually thought of as a dominant 7th (G7) type of sound. Because it contains no third (B♮ or B♭), it could be part of the dominant or minor chord families. "F" is the ♭7 of "G." When you superimpose a triad built from the ♭7 degree over a bass note, that triad supplies the ♭7th, 9th, and 11th chord tones which gives us G9(11) or Gm9(11). The 11th degree can also be referred to as the 4th or as a suspension: G9sus or Gm9sus.

One additional thought I'd like to add. You will hear these kinds of "slash" chords (F/G) referred to, incorrectly, as poly-chords. A poly-chord refers to harmony where two or more chords are actually being played simultaneously. You will find this kind of fantastic harmony, most often, in 20th century classical music. Such harmony is extremely difficult to associate one mode or chord scale with, and as you can see, with the conventional "slash" chords presented here, they all readily give us either a diatonic scale/mode or familiar scale-type with which to improvise. A true poly-chord would not do that so easily.

Example 4:
triad superimposition chart

Major Triads

Triad/Root or Bass Note	Chord Name (most functional)	Mode/Scale
F triad/G	G7(9,11)	G Mixolydian, G Blues
F♯ triad/G	This sound can function like a V7(alt.) chord	G whole-tone/half-tone diminished [G] A [B♭] C [C♯] D♯ E [F♯] B Harmonic Minor B [C♯] D E [F♯] [G] [A♯]B
G triad/G	Gmaj	G Major, G Lydian
A♭ triad/G	Fm/G	G Phrygian
A triad/G	G7(13, 9, ♯11) or Gmaj7♯4(6, 9)	G Lydian ♭7 G Lydian
B♭ triad/G	Gm7	G Dorian
B triad/G	Gmaj7(♯5)	G Lydian Augmented
C triad/G	Cmaj/G This sound is used in many ways, and tends to help create a Gospel or Blues feeling	C Major, C Blues, C Lydian G Major, G Blues
D♭ triad/G	G7(♭9, ♭5)	G half-tone/whole-tone diminished [G] [A♭] B♭ B [D♭] D E [F]
D triad/G	Gmaj7(9)	G Major, G Lydian
E♭ triad/G	Cm7/G	C Dorian
E triad/G	G7(13, ♭9)	G half-tone/whole-tone diminished [G] [G♯] B♭ [B] D♭ D [E] F

Minor Triads

Triad/Root or Bass Note	Chord Name (most functional)	Mode/Scale
Fm triad/G	Fm/G	G Phrygian
F♯m triad/G	Gmaj7(♯4, 9)	G Lydian
Gm triad/G	Gm	G Dorian
A♭m triad/G	G7(♯5, ♭9)	G Altered Dominant Super Locrian
Am triad/G	C6/G This is a sound used a lot in Gospel music	G Major, G Mixolydian, G Blues
B♭m triad/G	Gm7♭5	G Locrian/B♭ Dorian
Bm triad/G	Gmaj7	G Major, G Lydian
Cm triad/G	Cm/G	C Dorian
D♭m triad/G	G7(13, ♭9, ♭5)	G half-tone/whole-tone diminished
Dm triad/G	G7(9)	G Mixolydian, G Blues
E♭m triad/G	G♭13(♭9)/G ♭9 in bass (rarely used)	G♭ half-tone/whole-tone diminished
Em triad/G	G6	G Major, G Mixolydian, G Blues

triad usage

I've tried to present one comprehensive example of just how you might go about using major or minor triads in the context of a common chord progression (I–vi7–ii7–V7). Let's examine what I might play, we'll just assume that this would blend with keyboards and the rest of the arrangement. If you have a problem understanding the theory behind why I've selected any of these triads try to figure it out yourself by building up each chord from the root in thirds and then label each major or minor triad. If that proves difficult consult with a musical friend or your teacher.

The first chord is named Ebmaj7 but as you can see, all I've chosen to play is a G-minor triad (G, Bb, and D), the 3rd, 5th, and maj 7th of Eb. There are times when an arranger would name this chord Gm/Eb because he/she wants to make sure that you play a triad, with some experience, you'll probably just know to do that by instinct. The next chord is Cm7, here I'm just playing an Eb triad (Eb, G, Bb), the b3rd, 5th, and b7th of C. Over the Fm7, I play an Ab triad, with the reasoning being the same. In bars 4 and 12, the inversion of the Ab triad remains but is now played over a Bb bass note making the chord a Bb9(sus). On the last chord of those bars, you'll notice that the top voice moves for voice leading purposes. For greater harmonic interest and to create tension, in bar 8 on the third beat, I played E/Bb which gives us Bb7(b5,b9). In bar 16, with the principle being the same but to add variety, I played G/Bb to realize a Bb13(b9) and here I used descending chromatic voice leading. This was more easily accomplished as I used a slightly higher inversion of the Ab/Bb chord.

Example 5: Triad Usage 🔊 Track 2

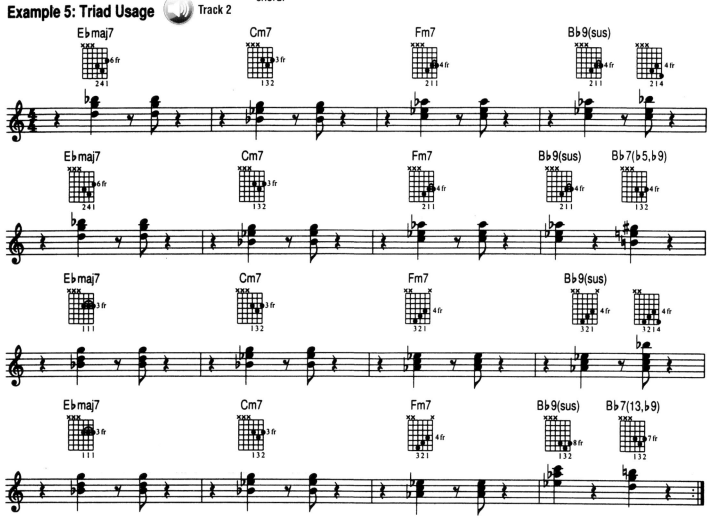

In most cases, an arranger (if there is one) will not write out what your top note should be, so it's up to you and your sense of harmony and good taste. The more you're called upon to do this, the better your instincts will become as to just what is the right thing to play. If you were to turn the suggested top notes into half-notes or quarter-notes and sing them aloud with full rhythmic value, they should form a nice, though simple, long melody. Give it a try! This style of guitar accompaniment is usually found in R&B (rhythm and blues), Pop, and various forms of "dance" music. There's a lot more to doing it with improvised grace and logic than you might imagine.

guide tones derivation

It's certainly understandable that you would be eager to skip right to the most modern harmonic concepts, but it will all make more sense, and pay greater dividends, if we begin with far more basic musical formations. I'm speaking of 2-note "guide tones," simple intervals of 4ths, 5ths, and tritones (♯4ths or ♭5ths) which, when placed above the root clearly define the chord family and outline the harmony. In serving this function they also provide a basic harmonic backdrop without making the soloist a prisoner of YOUR concepts!

The guide tone chart looks at the three basic chord families and views them on the guitar from the perspective of the root (located on either the "A" or "E" string and voiced functionally from there). On the left side, you see a full 4-note chord, then to the right, with the root and one other pitch removed. The guide tones remain. When played in the context of a iim7-V7-I or a iim7(♭5)-V7-i progression, it's obvious how smoothly these simple harmonic forms flow into one another. As you progress through the materials presented here, the guide tones will invariably serve as our building blocks. Always, a "can't go wrong" place to start, especially when reading through a tune for the first time.

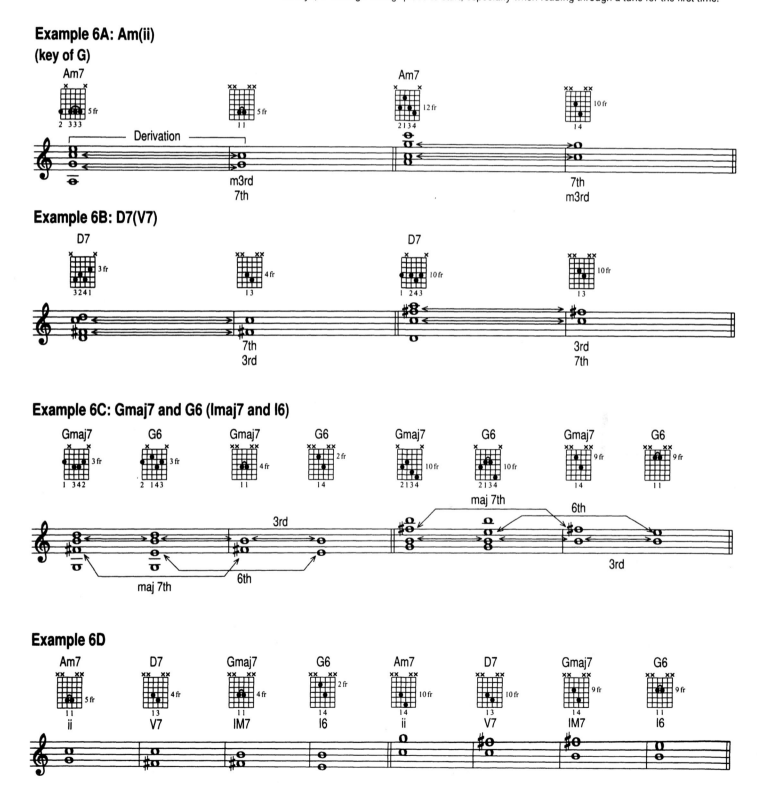

Example 6A: Am(ii)
(key of G)

Example 6B: D7(V7)

Example 6C: Gmaj7 and G6 (Imaj7 and I6)

Example 6D

Example 6E: Am7(♭5)(iiø)

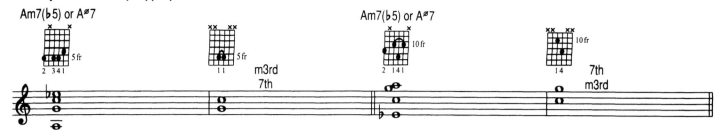

Example 6F

Clockwise from top left: John Scofield, Bill Connors, John Abercrombie, and Steve.
Taken at John Abercrombie's Manhattan loft, January 5th, 1984. Photo: Jonathan Postal

guide tone blues

There can be little argument that blues, in all its varied forms, is the common ground. A language spoken by players of all musical styles. In the blues form, the guide tones function with subtlety and crispness, seeming to urge the groove along. It's a style that fits into any instrumentation, but none better than the classic organ trio. Just check out Kenny Burrell on any of Jimmy Smith's great recordings for Blue Note or Verve.

In the following example, I've tried to present all the basics in two positions (lower and upper inversions), essentially with the intervals inverted, always using the "D" and "G" strings for maximum warmth, punch, and uniformity of sound and tone color.

Example 7: Lower Inversions Track 4

Example 8: Upper Inversions Track 4

Steve Khan

As we reach for more harmonic sophistication, the idea of the superimposed iim7 to each dominant 7th is introduced. When you improvise with these on your own, you should sense the harmony "opening up."

Example 11: Minor Blues 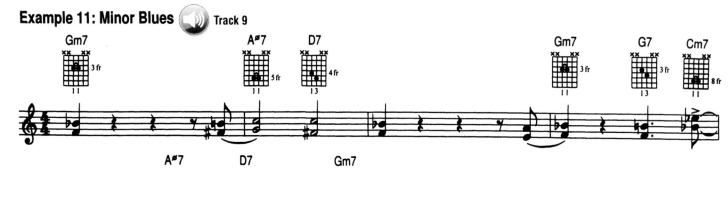 Track 9

Example 12: G Blues Track 4

suspended sounds — contemporary blues comping

How can we begin to break away from traditional approaches to blues harmony? The following two examples are offered as a conceptual and stylistic point of departure. Again, all the examples are presented over one of the most basic 12-bar blues progressions to allow the maximum amount of time to enjoy hearing each voicing. You may run into musicians and singers who will find this kind of harmonic approach as too pretty or too "jazzy" for their music. If such is the case, then on that job, go back to something more basic.

In Example 12, I've applied a iim7 chord (Dm7) over the root "G." (the basic chord sound is G7). This will invariably produce a suspended kind of sound and make the harmonic feeling very open, at times, lush and romantic.

Example 13 adds a little more depth while being rhythmically more active and percussive. This approach is based upon a guitar interpretation of McCoy Tyner's piano style. As in the previous examples, all chord sounds are the product of superimposing iim7 chords over the root of the dominant chord.

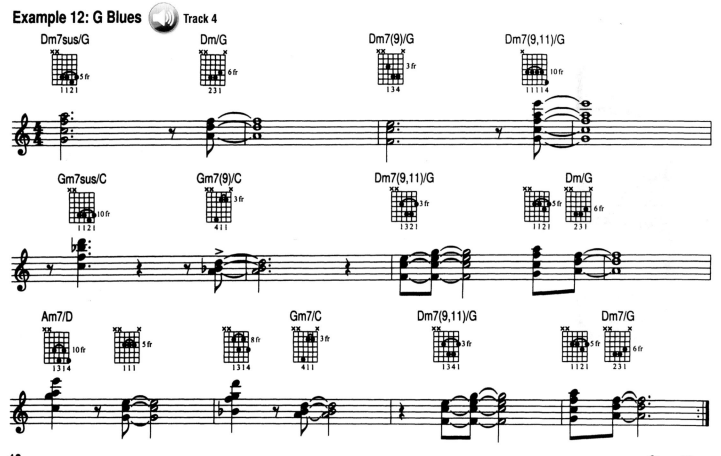

Steve Khan

Example 13: G Blues (Shuffle) Track 4

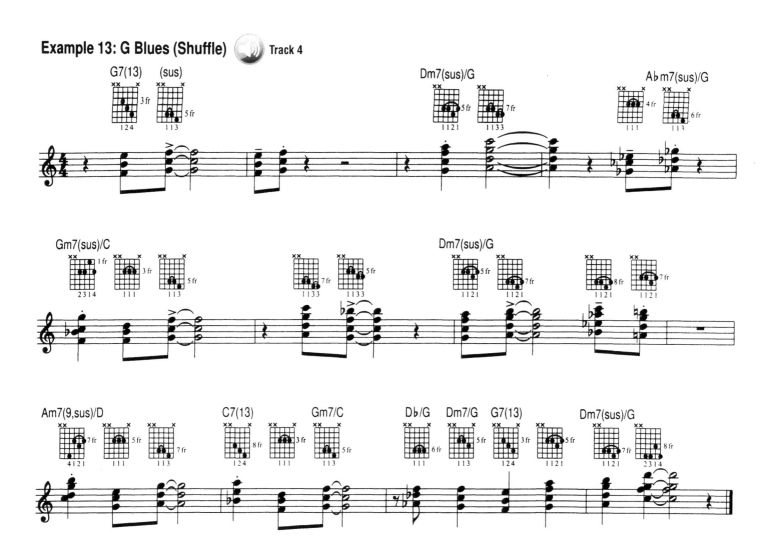

Eyewitness in Japan, left to right: Manolo Badrena, Anthony Jackson, Steve, and Steve Jordan.
Taken outside the Pit Inn, Tokyo, May 1983. Photo: Tatsuhiko Tanaka

jazz-type blues

The harmonic treatment of a 12-bar blues by a jazz oriented player will usually differ from the format we've been using for a basic blues, in that we've been making use of only the I7, IV7, and V7 chords. You will see and hear differences in the approach to bars 2, 4, 6, 8, and 9–12. Of special interest to me are bars 4 and 8. In bar 4, as we've already been playing over a I7 for the previous three bars, this is where our tonic becomes the dominant 7th (V7) to the IV chord. In the key of our example, F7 is going to resolve to Bb7. The jazz player takes advantage of this moment by adding a iim7 (Cm7) in front of the F7 to add more color, motion, and tension towards the eventual resolution. A familiar substitution/alteration in this process, generally associated with John Coltrane would be to use the b5 substitute for F7, which would be B7, and inserting a iim7 (F#m7), thus creating a different approach to final resolution. In a sense, you're approaching resolution from one-half step above. Just an alternate thought, what if you were to approach resolution from one-half step below? Haven't you ever done that while playing chords? You know, sliding up to the Bb7 from A7? What if you were to try and slip a iim7 chord in front of it? Or, use that modality to approach resolution with your lines. Thinking about things like this, prior to actually playing them, can give rise to musical creations, born of thought, which might actually sound great to you. Never any harm in trying!

Depending upon the color of the chord used in bar 9, that will go a long ways towards determining how you might treat bar 8. Whatever is agreed upon, bar 8 can be a VI7 (D7) chord resolving to either II7 (G7) or iim7 (Gm7). These same kinds of harmonic principles can also be applied to the 3-chord kind of blues we've been utilizing. We were, if you'll recall, using a G blues, so bar 9 was a D7 (V7) in that progression. So, it's possible that we could have treated bar 8 as an A7 (V7 of V7), but we could even try to employ an E7 (VI7). Here, however, we're using a bit of our imagination as E7 is a V7 of Am7 which we have been superimposing over the D7 to extend the harmony so why couldn't this work too? In transcribing solos by many past masters, I've seen their lines imply this change even when the bass and keyboards were not. Again, give it a try and see what happens.

Example 14: Blues in F 🔊 Track 11

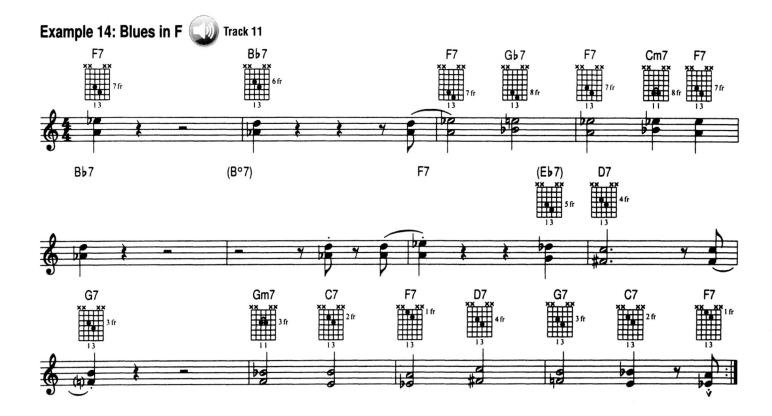

Steve Khan

jazz blues with common tone chordal punctuations

One of the most powerful lessons I've taken away from all my Wes Montgomery listening and transcribing was his orchestral (big band like) conception of the guitar. Whether he was soloing or comping behind Mel Rhyne and Jimmy Smith, it seemed as though his high 3-note voicings were acting like a trumpet section. His mid-register 2-, 3-, and 4-note chords were like the saxophone section, and when he'd riff with octaves behind the soloist, it sounded like trombones; thus giving the guitar remarkable scope and color. Perhaps he would not have verbalized this concept in the same manner, but I find this to be an effective way of expressing what I heard and still hear in his playing.

One method for getting a grip on this concept is to punctuate your guide tones with chord voicings utilizing a top note on your high "E" string. It's great for your developing ears to try and maintain a common tone in your top voice as often as is possible. It also helps to hear how beautifully harmony moves, and how efficient harmonic motion on the guitar can be.

An additional, and valuable, practice tool would be to use a kind of octave displacement in your top voice. For example, in a "G" blues, play a voicing with "D" as your top note on the "B" string. Then answer that with "D" as the top note of a chord on the high "E" string. As the chord progression moves along try to get "D" on top of each chord if you can. Once you get the hang of it, you will be able to comp with a big band concept, with all three sections under your fingers.

Example 15   Track 11

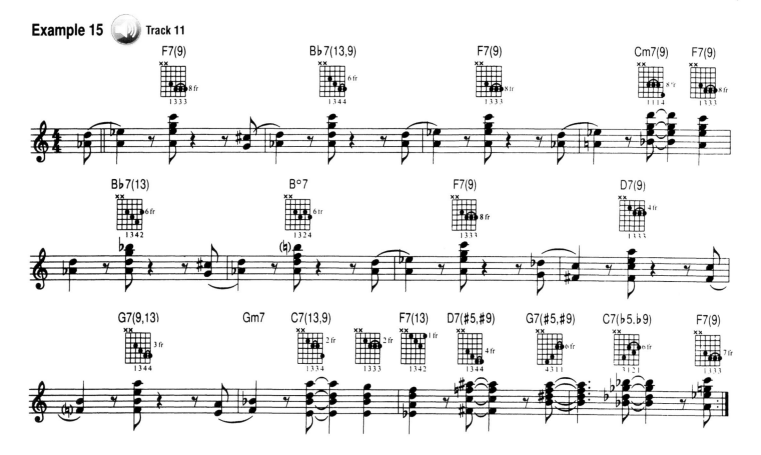

turnarounds

This brings us to discussing bars 11 and 12, in a jazz-type blues most players will put to use either a I7–VI7–II7–V7 or I7–VI7–iim7–V7 progression (2 beats per chord). I'm presenting examples in both "F" and "G," if you were to be playing with, at the very least, a bassist, you would usually not use the notes given on the low "E" and "A" strings. However, in my attempt to cover as much material as possible, I wanted to make sure that, for those of you who have heard guitarists sound like they're both the guitar AND the bass, you have gained a sense of how this is done. Perhaps my favorite example of this style (essentially it's guide tones with a bass note) was recorded by Jim Hall and Bill Evans on their version of "My Funny Valentine" from *Undercurrents* (Blue Note/Solid State). Each part (the bass line and the guide tones) could certainly function on its own, but here it's a new challenge to try and play both. The trick, fingering-wise, is the constant shifting of the 1st and 2nd fingers on your left-hand (if your pick is held in your right-hand). If you were not playing the bass notes, all the minor 7th guide tones would be played with your 1st finger only, and all the dominant 7th guide tones would be played with your 1st and 3rd fingers. As a discipline, just try playing the bass lines by themselves and gain a feeling for how a bass player might approach such a line.

Example 16A: Blues Turnaround in F (Upper Inversions)

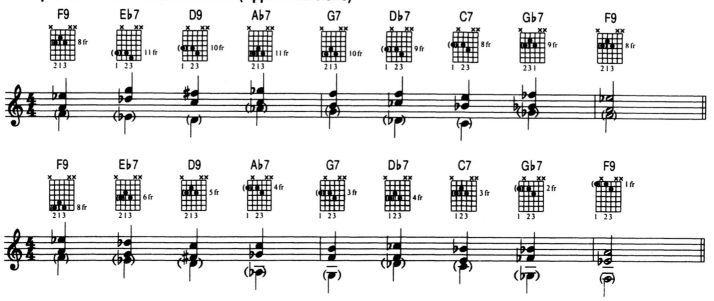

Example 16B: Turnaround in G Major

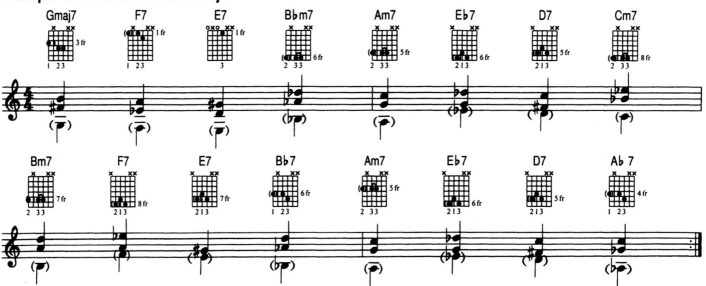

Steve Khan

rhythm and blues/ gospel chordal approach

Though I wouldn't dare attempt to posture myself as a complete historian on the growth of gospel music's chordal style and its deep rooted place in American popular music, I am certain that I have a good feeling for this music. And, always keep in mind that no matter how far out you may aspire to play, the blues should always be present somewhere in your music.

The reference sheet which follows (Example 17) is offered simply as a place to begin. As you'll notice, on the guitar (like the right-hand of a pianist), the style is rooted in simple major, minor, diminished, and augmented triads. If you'd like to delve deeper into the style from a pianists' point of view, make the effort to watch and listen to the videos and recordings of Ray Charles, Richard Tee, and Dr. John.

With two sample choruses of a 12-bar "G" blues (Examples 18 and 19), I've tried to give you most of the basics as I might employ them. Obviously one could devote an entire text to this area alone, but I hope that this will inspire you to explore this wonderful genre at greater length. I've also offered an alternate introduction, or pick-up, in the style of Wes Montgomery because he did so many clever things with his blues oriented compositions, especially in his usage of parallel diminished 7th chords.

Example 17: Derivation of Gospel / Rhythm & Blues Chordal Style

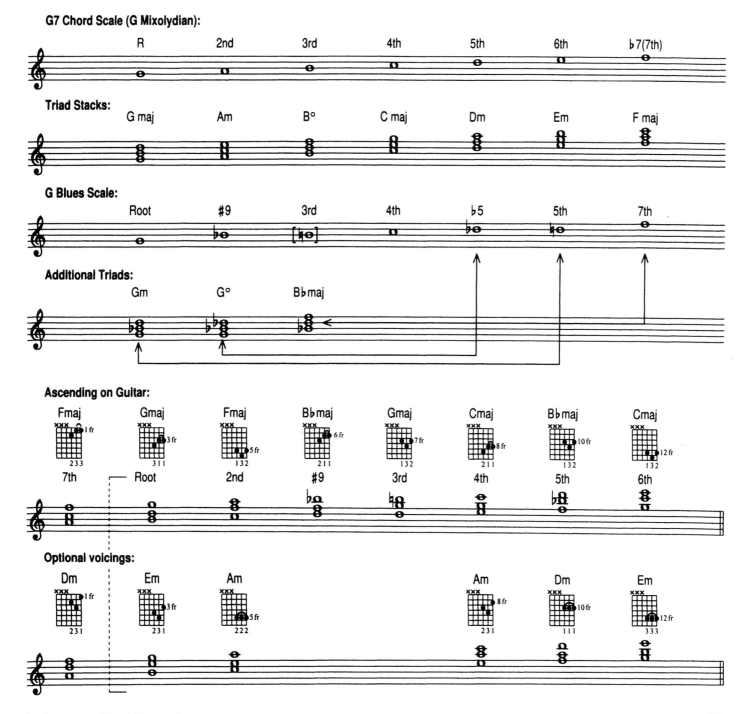

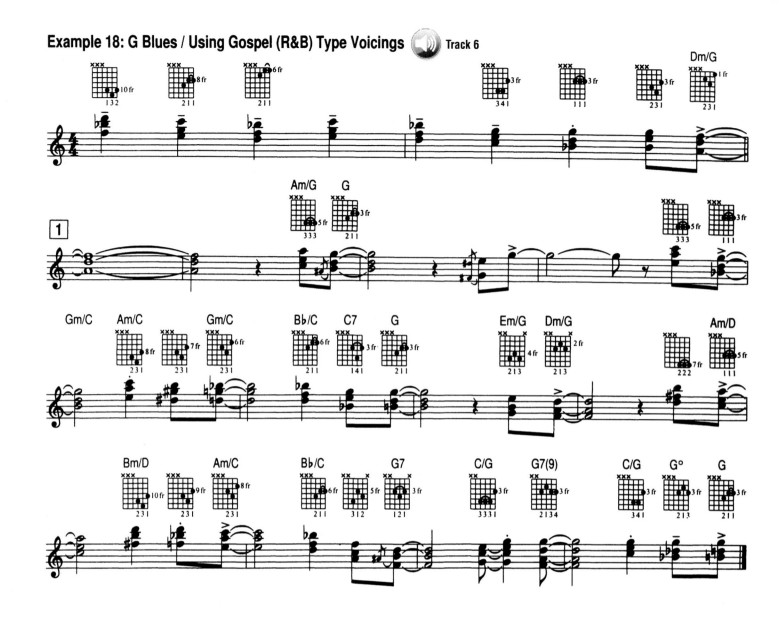

Perhaps the most often-used cadence in Gospel music is the aptly labeled "Amen Cadence." It can appear in a variety of forms, including: IV–I, IV7–I, IV7–I7, iv–I, and iv7–I. These would be used as an alternative to more basic V–I cadence. In the key of G, it could appear simply as C to G or even C/G to G. When playing over a blues or perhaps, better yet for practice purposes, a G pedal, you'll find that a back-and-forth motion between simple triads will create mini-cadences. I've already mentioned C to G and C/G to G, another variation of that would be G to Am/G and back to G. You could view the Am as a function of C6/G, so, it too generates an Amen feeling. The sense of momentary resolution could also be created with this motion: G to Bb/G to C/G, then back to Bb/G, and finally resting on G. Remember, just let the bass do ITS job playing the bass notes and you concentrate on the colors created by the triads. Let them speak! Finally, though this creates a dominant 7th oriented feeling, it's very common to start with the sound of Dm/G moving to Em/G and then returning to rest on Dm/G. I hope that sharing these simple concepts in the text will help your own analysis of Examples 18–19 as well as the reference chart presented in Example 17. You will hear all of these concepts put to use in the improvised example, "Don Grolnelius" located on Track [33] and performed in the key of C.

Example 19 🔊 Track 6

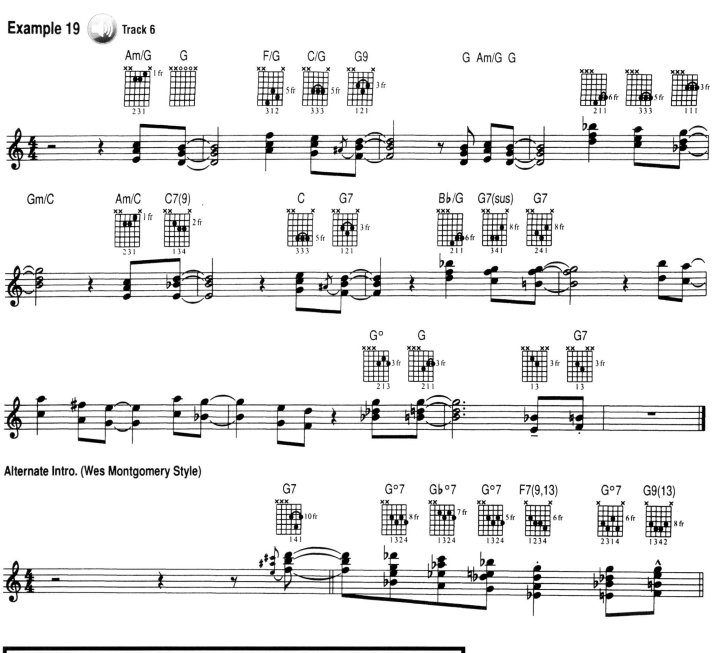

Alternate Intro. (Wes Montgomery Style)

Steve with Wes Montgomery at the Hollywood Bowl Concert, ca. 1966.
Original Polaroid: Sammy Cahn

**harmony built
across the strings**

We will now build chords, one voice at a time, using the guide tones as a starting point. You've already begun by using your "D" and "G" strings for the guide tone lines (examples 20, 23, 26 and 29). Next you will add a voice on your "B" string (examples 21, 24, 27 and 30). Once that is understood, you will add voices on both your "B" and "E" strings (examples 22, 25, 28 and 31).

Basic voice leading principles as you add voices across the strings:

1. Try to keep a common tone in your top voice as the chords shift;

2. Try to move the top voice chromatically up or down as YOU hear the harmony shifting.

While attending U.C.L.A., I felt I was so far behind my classmates that I sought extra help with private piano harmony and theory lessons from a classical instructor. She tried very hard to have me understand the concept of "the will of the tone." At the time, I just didn't get it. Perhaps because her orientation was to communicate to me in a classical harmonic language and not with a Pop, Rock, or Jazz vocabulary which might have found a better connection with me.

If you observe the movement of the guide tones as the V7 resolves to the tonic, the intervals of the 3rd and ♭7, within the dominant 7th chord, seem as though they MUST resolve. The 3rd "must" resolve to the root of the tonic, and the ♭7 "must" resolve to the major or minor 3rd. Thus, with only two voices, the harmony is clearly defined and those voices now do seem to have a "will" of their own. Play the next example. Listen for how the 3rd and ♭7th of the F7 chord "pull" towards the tonic and 3rd of the B♭ chord.

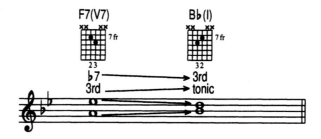

When you add alterations (♯5, ♭5, ♯9, ♭9) as chromatic passing tones, you might want to make sure that the movement of the pitches is reflected in how you choose to "spell" the chord. By this I mean, using sharps to indicate ascending motion and flats for descending movement. In choosing one or the other, you might be indicating that the ♯5 of the dominant will resolve up to the 3rd of the tonic. But the ♭13 might resolve down to the 9th of the tonic. Our system of music notation is not that strict when it comes to the labeling of chords, but for the sake of clear communication it is something to think about. After all, you want a piece of music played as you hear it as soon as possible and clear communication in your writing speeds up that process.

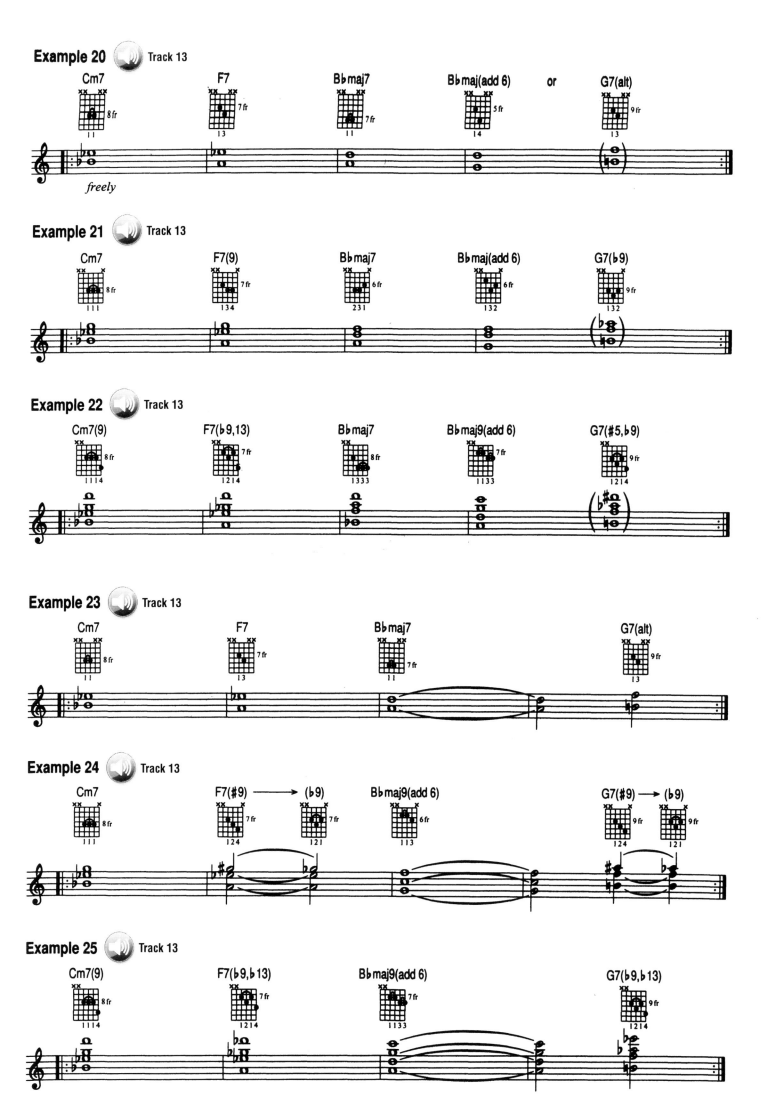

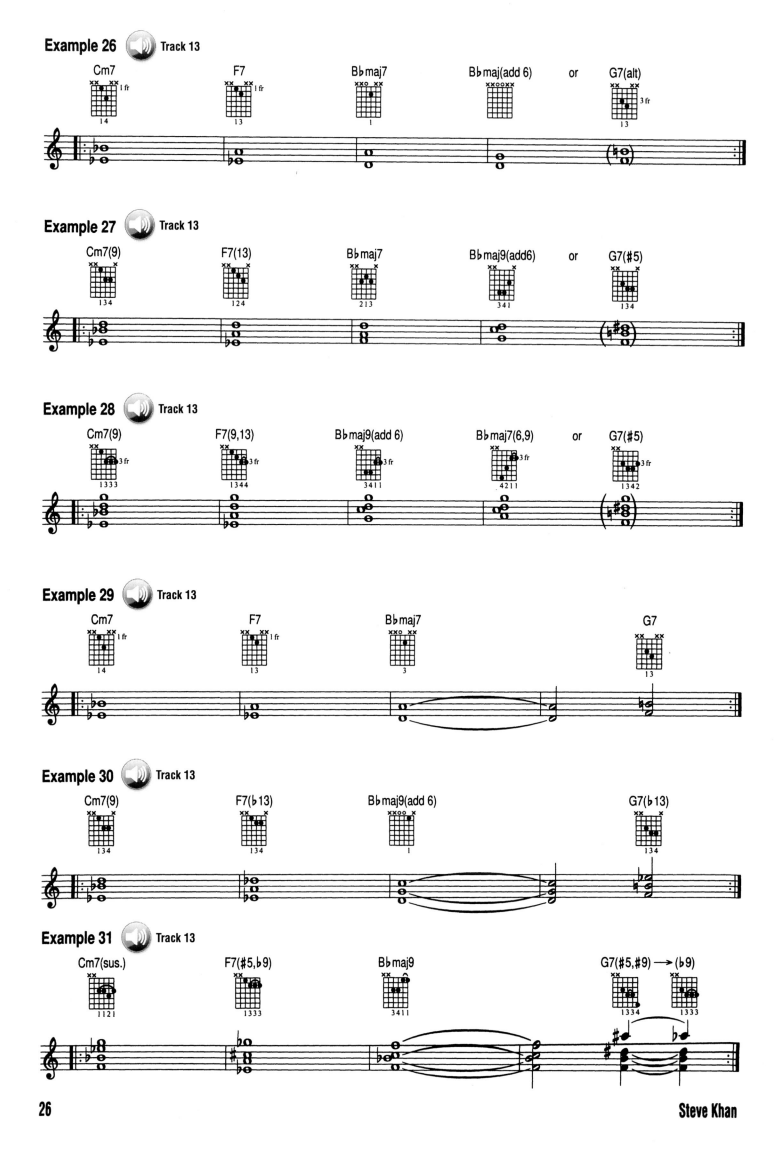

iim7–V7–I–V7 over a pedal

Sometimes a great music lesson can come from a most unexpected source. In the early years of my career, I accompanied many "pop" music singers. Often in such a setting, the basic rhythm section is augmented by a full orchestra (5 trumpets, 4 trombones, 5 reeds, plus strings). For chordal instruments, especially the guitar, it can be a great learning experience to be forced to see and hear that PLAYING LESS can be SAYING MORE!

In any given performance, there would almost always be a moment when the singer would tell a story over a LONG vamp, sometimes this vamp was over a pedal point (one static pitch from the bassist). As I would sit amongst the orchestra and listen, I could hear the chords moving even though the bass was only playing a single note. The pedal was invariably the root of the V7 chord, and all the harmonies sounded beautiful over this one note. Truly this was a great arranger's device.

In this series of examples, I've presented everything in the key of C major; therefore, we will use a "G" pedal under the entire progression. We begin with Example 32 utilizing just the guide tones which supply the basic harmonic movement in the progression. In Example 33, we add a third voice on the "B" string, attempting to maintain a common-tone top voice as an ear-training discipline. Adding a fourth voice on the "E" string, in Examples 34, the common tone principle on the top voice remains. When this is not possible, the top voice should move in a manner dictated by where our ears seem to lead us.

Examples 35 and 36 extend the concept by introducing ascending and descending chromatic movement in the top-voice. As a discipline, I've attempted to make this voice move in half-steps whenever possible. Always keep in mind that I've just chosen ONE option. You have many choices and, after a time, your own style of harmony will dictate YOUR choices.

When you feel that you are comfortable with these exercises over the "G" pedal, try to transpose the ideas to work over the "C" pedal provided on the recording. Since the "C" pedal is the root of a dominant chord you'll be in the key of "F," and the movement would take you through Gm7–C7–Fmaj7–D7(alt.). When you're practicing, rehearsing, or jamming with a bassist and drummer, try this concept as an extended introduction to a standard, or perhaps one of your own original tunes.

Most of the exercises in this book are presented in the form of whole notes. I feel that it's important to grow accustomed to the beauty of long tones as the harmony slowly moves through the chords. Long notes on the guitar can, at times, be just as effective as the short percussive strokes with which we guitarists are most associated.

Eyewitness in 1989. Clockwise from lower left: Anthony Jackson, Manolo Badrena, Steve, and Dave Weckl. Original Ned Shaw pencil sketch for "PUBLIC ACCESS" CD cover.

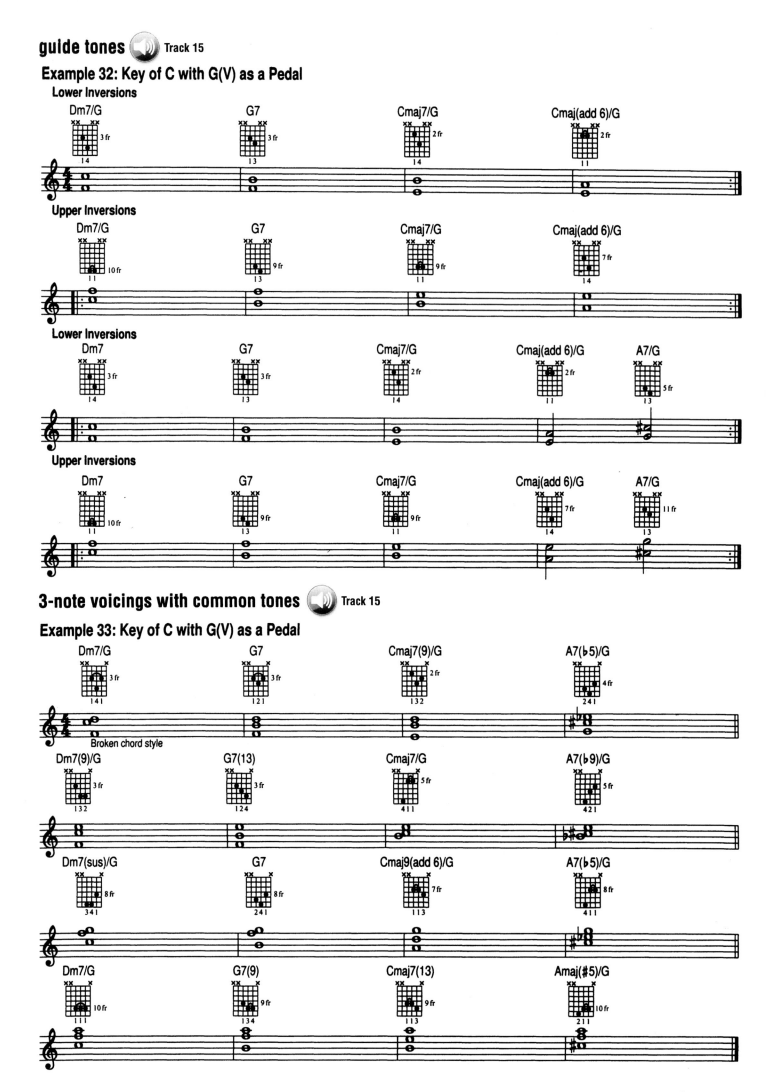

Example 32: Key of C with G(V) as a Pedal

Lower Inversions

Upper Inversions

Lower Inversions

Upper Inversions

3-note voicings with common tones Track 15

Example 33: Key of C with G(V) as a Pedal

Broken chord style

4-note voicings with common tones Track 15

Example 34: Key of C with G(V) as a Pedal

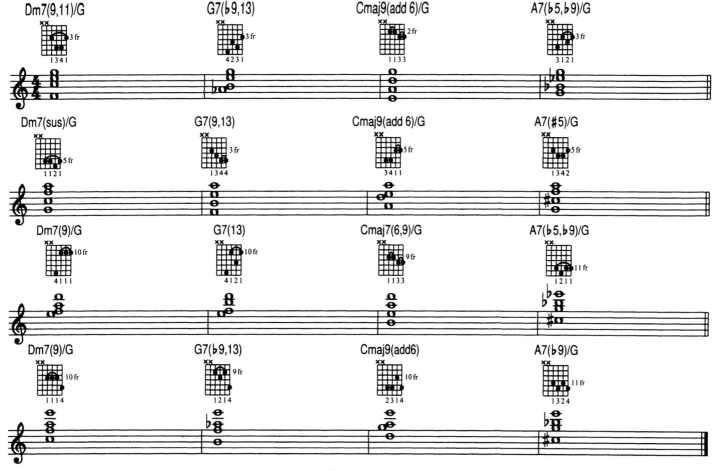

3- and 4-note voicings with chromaticism Track 15

Example 35: Key of C with G(V) as a Pedal

Ascending

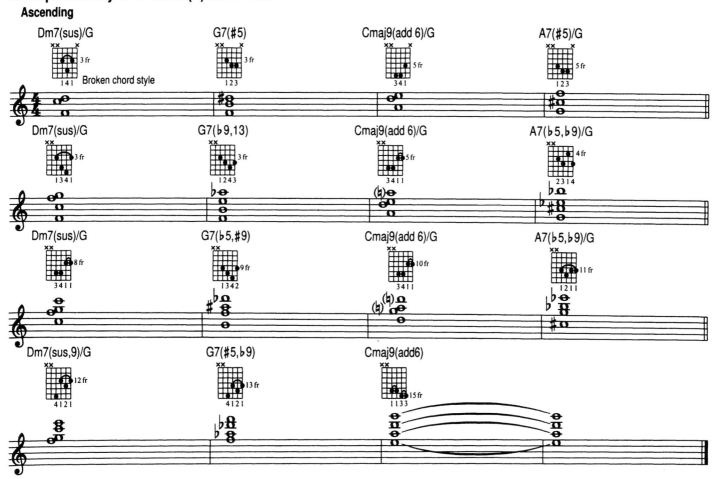

Example 36: Key of C with G(V) as a Pedal

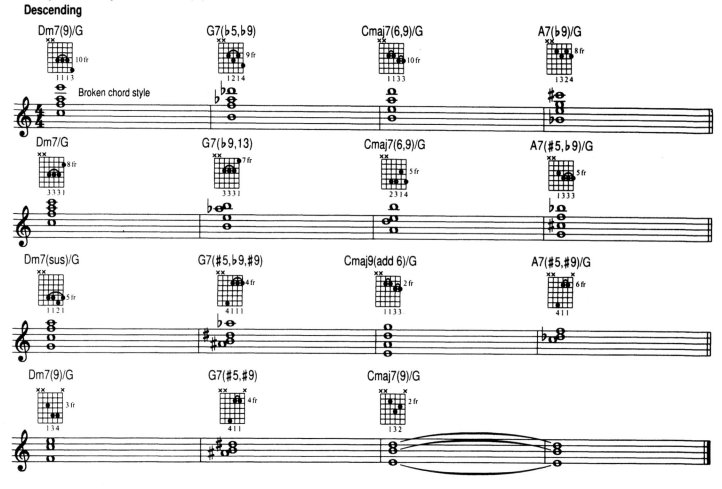

Playing for pass-the-hat at the Focus Gallery Coffee House just after arriving in New York City, 1970.
Trio dates were with John Miller (bass), and David Friedman (vibes).

Steve Khan

modes in chords

In assembling my studies for presentation, my goal is that you'll someday enjoy the same improvisational fluency with chords as you now do with your improvised lines. I've chosen to pass along the manner in which I approached solving this problem for myself. Having offered this method many, many times to private students, and in clinics and seminars, I have seen it work, and I'm sure that you'll see its particular kind of logic and follow through with the work.

We begin by separating the three chord families: dorian (minor), mixolydian (dominant), and lydian (major). When I did this for myself, it was my hope that if I could improvise upon one isolated family, and hear melodies with chords, I would be able to do the same when faced with harmony in motion perhaps having less time to observe each passing chord.

The following examples are presented so that the first row contains common voicings; as you scan down the page the options become more sophisticated. Each example is presented in "G" (G dorian, G mixolydian and G lydian). The top voice of each chord is on the "E" string, with each note of the mode being harmonized with a modal chord voicing. Generally speaking, the first two rows offer chord forms which guitarists are expected to know. Beneath certain pitches, two options can be seen as being standard.

I want to take a moment and discuss the major chord family and why the lydian mode will be the scale of choice throughout this text. If we continue, for purposes of discussion, to use "G" as our root, then you should know that the "G" ionian mode is the "G" major scale (G, A, B, C, D, E, F♯). The notes in the "G" lydian mode (G, A, B, C♯, D, E, F♯) differ only in that the 4th degree of the scale is C♯ instead of C. So, why choose one over the other? It's purely a choice of sound by convention. For the most part, this choice usually appears in jazz and pop-standard song contexts. In most rock, country, and folk styles the ♮4th of the major scale/ionian mode is most appropriate. When you're playing, your choice should be based upon what you hear as sounding best for the music!

As you grow more familiar with the basics, all you would have to do, when putting any of the reference charts to use, is look straight down the page, follow the columns connecting the voicings with a common top-note and your sonic options would begin to grow. What should eventually develop is that these voicings become familiar "sound shapes" and NOT just some chords you know. You will end up HEARING how you use these sound shapes and, in being able to hear that, you'll find your freedom.

When playing in pop, rock, or R&B contexts, especially where a vocalist is involved, there will be times when you must harmonize the melody note which is sung. If the note is in one of these three chord families, you have an at-hand reference for finding the sound shape which might fit the harmonic style of your group.

In an instrumental setting, you may want to add harmony to a specific note in the melody of an original tune or a standard. These three chord family charts should provide you with most of the basic voicings and those which offer more color tones.

The standard practice method to employ here is to choose any one of the chord families for work at a particular sitting and while playing along with the sample "G" pedal, go up and down the mode in chords, playing them in long tones (whole notes at least) until they seem to fall easily under your fingers. A vital secondary aspect to your practice regimen would be to sing along with the top voice of each chord so that its melodic aspect begins to be a part of the way you HEAR the voicing. Then, like with your single-note lines, you'll be that much closer to playing what you hear and that's where you want to be.

Example 37: Basic Voicings (G Dorian)

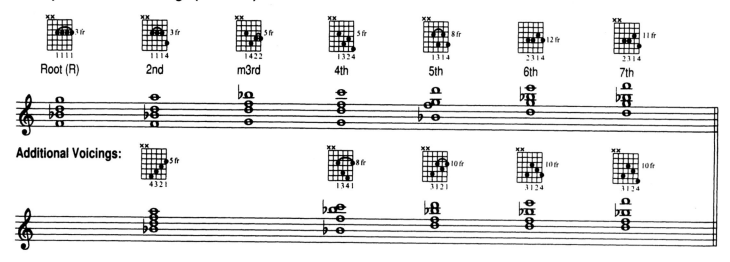

Additional Voicings:

Voicings with more Color Tones:

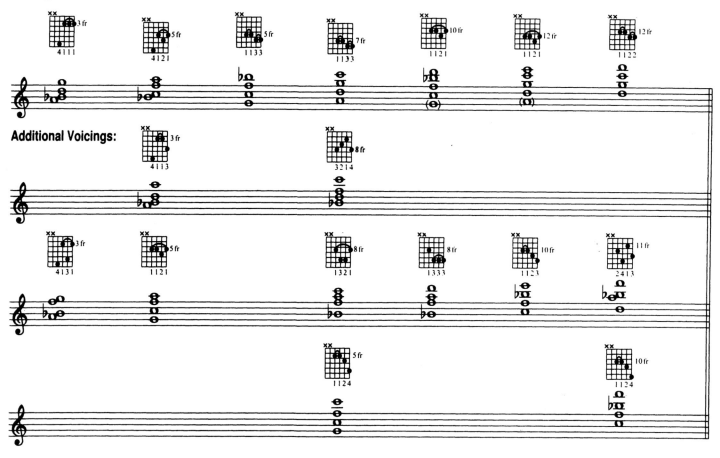

Additional Voicings:

Steve Khan

Example 38: Basic Voicings (G Mixolydian)

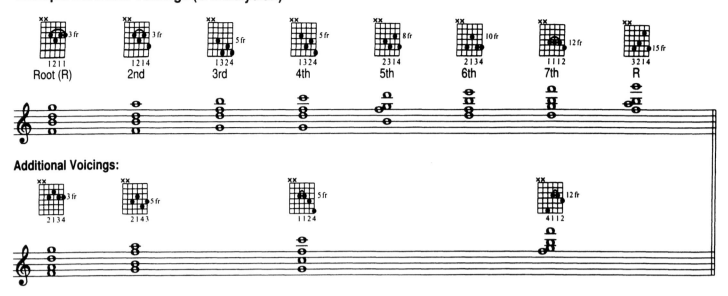

Additional Voicings:

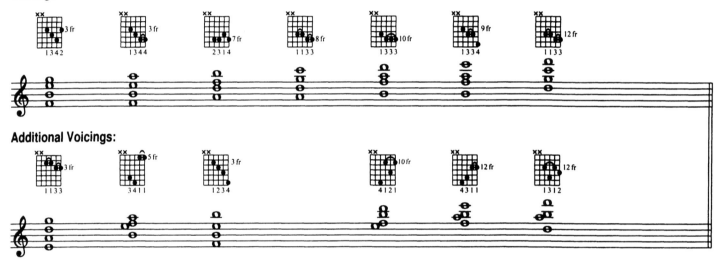

Voicings with more Color Tones:

Additional Voicings:

Lost in America on tour with the Brecker Brothers.
Photo taken by Charisse Taylor in a hotel room, "Anywhere," U.S.A., 1976

Example 39: Basic Voicings (G Lydian)

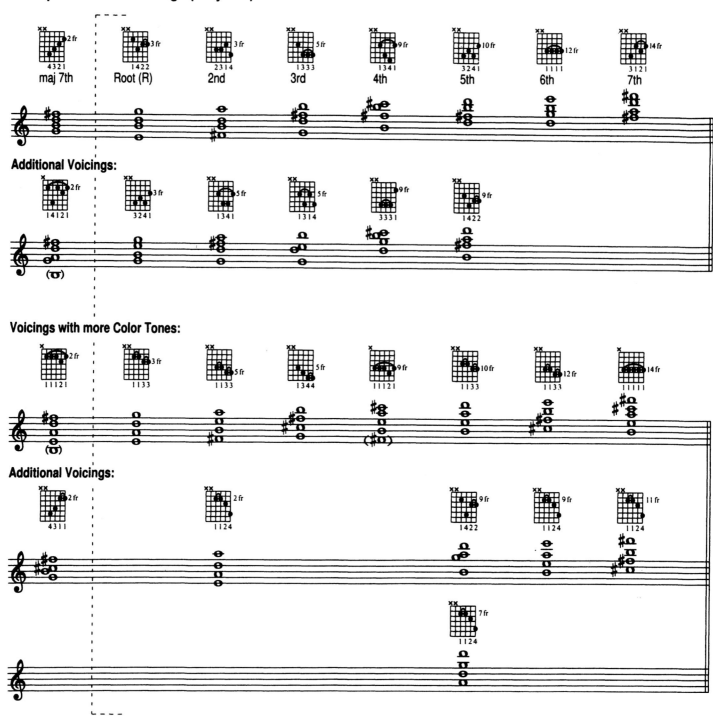

basic 3-note voicings (g dorian)

Example 39A: Minor 7 Chord Family (G minor 7)

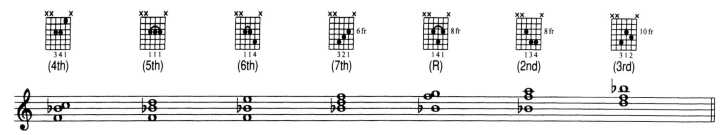

basic 3-note voicings (c mixolydian)

Example 39B: Dominant 7 Chord Family (C7)

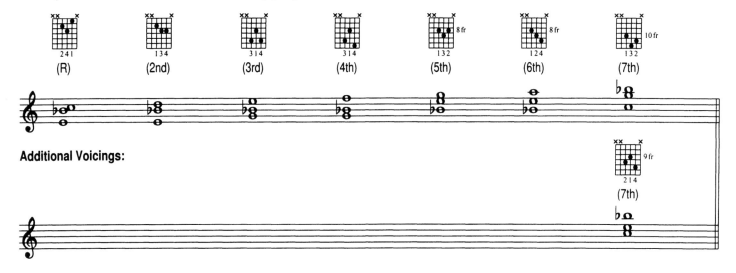

basic 3-note voicings (f lydian)

Example 39C: Major 7 Chord Family (F Major 7)

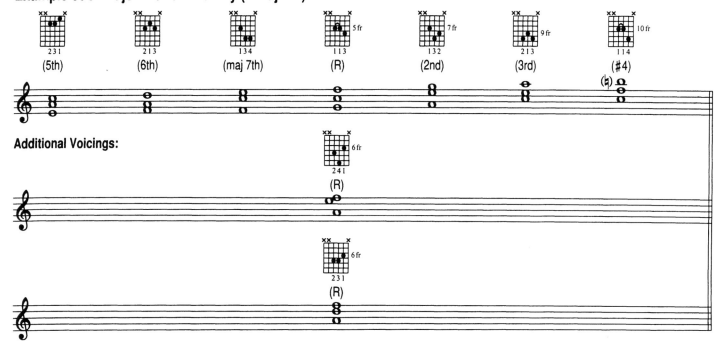

chordal study derived from a linear exercise

While developing a practice regimen which accelerates your growth, I believe you'll find that hearing what you practice will enable you to eventually play what you hear. While learning to feel free with chords, you can always count on taking the simplest of linear practice ideas (right from your earliest scale and modal work) and apply it at half-speed, so to speak, with the top-voice moving in chords as the line would.

Use Example 40 as an illustration. Example 40 is a sequential line in F major (G dorian and C mixolydian are modes in that family with the exact same notes) which goes up a 3rd and down a step, up a 3rd, etc. This melody is then harmonized with the different voicings in Examples 41–44. Use the "G" pedal on the recording and play each chord slowly. It can really help if you sing the top note out loud (even if you don't have a good voice, this will pay off down the road).

Example 40

Example 41 uses basic shapes and Example 42 adds chords with more color tones. It's essential that you take the time to do the same work with the remaining two basic chord families: G major (G lydian) and G dominant 7th (G mixolydian).

Examples 43 and 44 are intended for use over the C pedal as if we were improvising over an extended C dominant 7th vamp. Here I've presented how once the dominant 7th "feeling" and "sound" has been established, the superimposition of iim7 (Gm7) chords serves to open up the sound. Example 43 uses basic chord forms and Example 44 brings in the color tones

Example 41: Chordal Exercise Using Sequence  Track 17

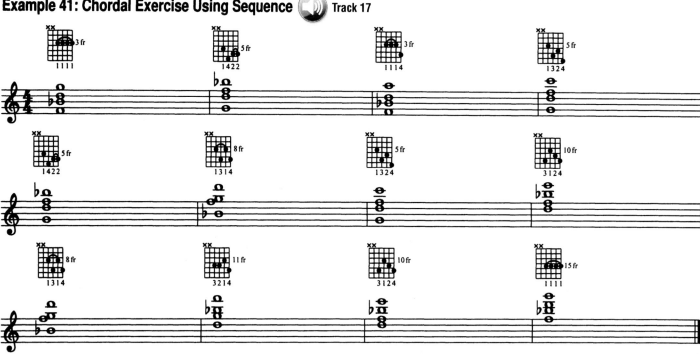

Example 42 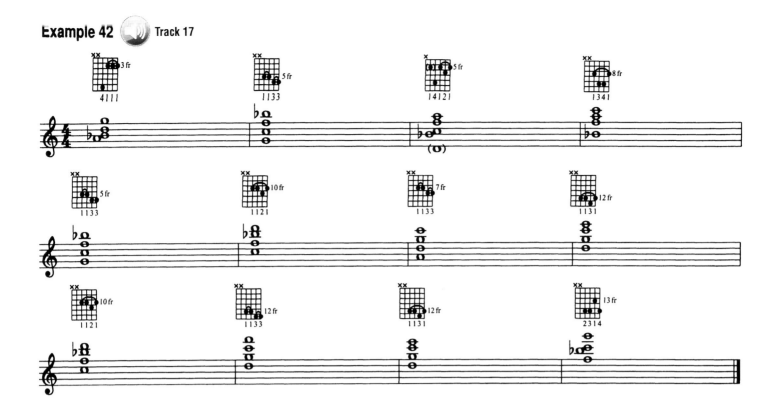 Track 17

Example 43 Track 17

Use over G Pedal or C Pedal

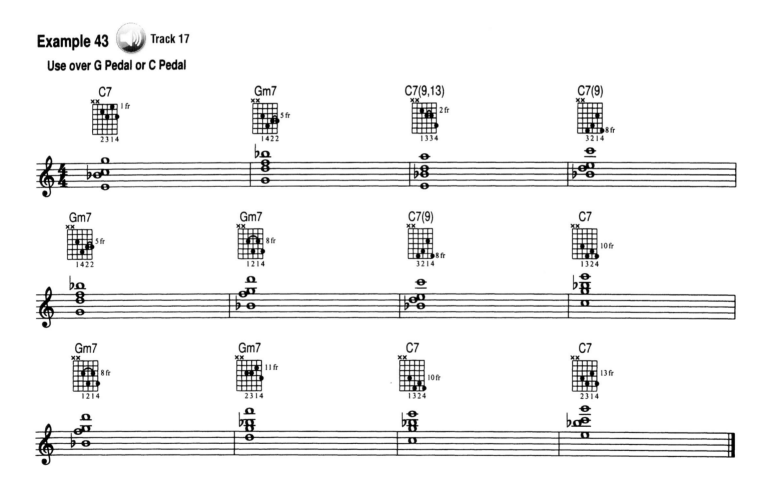

Example 44 🔊 Track 17

Use over G Pedal or C Pedal

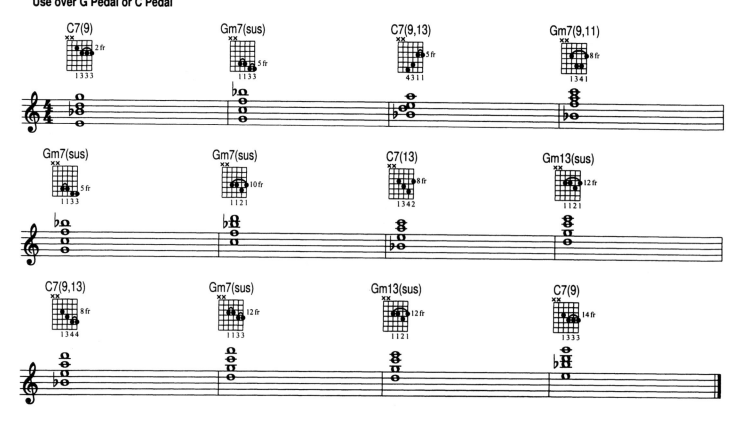

Publicity photo taken at David Tan's studio in Manhattan, ca. 1983–1985.

Steve Khan

style

Though it's my feeling that arriving at your own style will not be at the exclusion of any of your options, making a deep stylistic commitment to some style will be important.

So as food for thought, I've presented three examples used with the dominant 7th chord family. As time goes by, you might want to weigh your options within the major and minor chord families as well.

Bass Vamp

This example offers a common and simple guitar approach which is essentially rooted in the inherent blues quality of the instrument:

Example 45: Simple Guitar Style **Track 19**

Here we extend the harmonic territory with small clusters (closed voiced chords) in the style of pianist, Bill Evans. There are those who might find this approach for blues-based material as "too pretty." Listen and see what you think!

Example 46: Bill Evans Style (Closed Voicing) **Track 19**

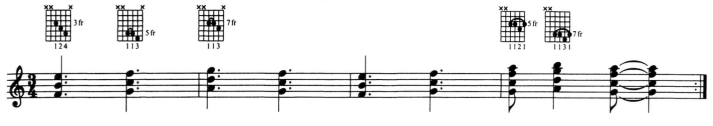

This example is in the style of McCoy Tyner's left-hand concept. These types of fingerings are called "open voicings." In a sense, this style should open-up the harmonic feeling, but, I find that Example 46 can accomplish this as well. There will be those who find the Tyner approach to be too "Far East" sounding due to all the 4ths in the chords. Again, listen and decide for yourself.

At any stage of your development, you will not be able to totally escape your influences. Should you be lucky enough to truly develop your own voice and style, I believe it will be accomplished when you're not trying so hard to consciously break free of your influences. It's my feeling, and especially where your harmonic concept is concerned, that at some point, you must make a commitment to the shapes of your lines and the chordal and harmonic sense you hear along with those lines. This is true even if, as guitarists, we don't accompany ourselves in a trio setting as a pianist does with their left-hand. It's important before playing to remind yourself that, "THIS IS THE WAY I PLAY, AND THIS IS THE WAY I HEAR MAKING MUSIC!" The first person you have to convince of this is yourself, once you've done that, convincing your peers and listeners in general won't be such a difficult task.

Example 47: McCoy Tyner Style (Open Voicing) **Track 19**

McCoy Tyner left-hand style piano voicings

When I was trying to arrive at an approach to harmony on the guitar, I ended up finding my greatest inspiration from the keyboard. I did spend a lot of time studying the chordal concepts of many of the guitar's great masters before moving away. In making this choice, I simply chose the style to which I felt the most emotionally connected. Without a doubt, that style was McCoy Tyner's. Especially his consistently centered left-hand approach. As we've arrived at the '90s, there's hardly a keyboard improviser who hasn't been touched in some way by McCoy's playing. Along with McCoy Tyner, the individuality of Herbie Hancock, Chick Corea, Joe Zawinul, and Keith Jarrett has also touched this work.

In trying to pass along my approach in the most direct manner, I have isolated the three basic chord families: major, minor, and dominant. For you, in your practice, the idea would be to develop fluency by practicing playing over one chord family for extended periods of time. In doing this, you would be developing your own sense of hearing these "left-hand" voicings moving in a melodic and emotional way. What makes this kind of practice approach readily usable is that, in many contemporary jazz and rock settings, you're asked to improvise/solo/jam over one chord (usually minor or dominant). Whether or not it's a finite length (like 8 bars or 16 bars) or something that's totally open ended, extended improvising practice over a pedal will have you totally prepared for these situations.

Though countless hours were spent listening to McCoy's work with John Coltrane's legendary quartet, his own recordings for MCA/Impulse, Blue Note, and Milestone, and his work as a sideman on countless Blue Note classics, I've found that the left-hand aspect of his style remains consistent and classic.

I've tried to lay out what he might likely play (using "G" as a tonal center) when confronted with dominant, major, or minor chord sounds. The only non-McCoy contribution comes from listening to Chick Corea, especially his mid-sixties work as a sideman on numerous Latin-jazz recordings (Cal Tjader and Herbie Mann). On minor chords, in addition to the voicings in 4ths, Chick adds (in this key) a simple B♭ triad over the "G" bass (spelling out a simple Gm7 chord), but when thrown into the mix with the more open voicings, it adds something wonderful.

Try to remember that on the piano, the left-hand is usually not played too far above the area of middle "C." On guitar, I've found that you'll achieve a consistent tone by keeping these 3-note voicings played across the D–G–B strings. So, depending upon the root, your choices for what you'll play and where you'll play it become obvious.

Example 48: G7

Example 49: G minor 7

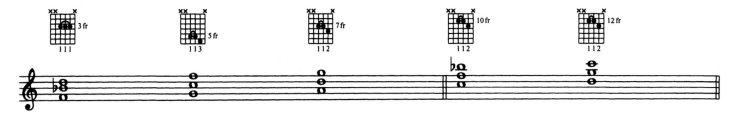

Example 50: G Major 7

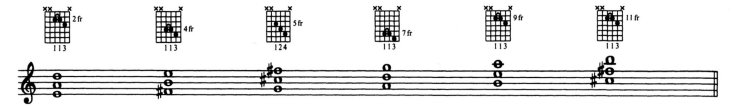

chord tones as melodies

In previous exercises, you've looked at such simple devices as common tone movement, chromatic top voice movement, octave displacement of the top voice, scale passages, and harmonized scale sequences for chords. Now, how about harmonizing chord tones and modal pitches as melodies.

To get the most out of this kind of exercise play the examples as single notes first. Then sing along with the melody. For the moment, allow yourself to believe that this is your melody. When it feels expressive to you, try adding the chordal suggestions I've supplied.

Here's a perfect opportunity to make use of one, or all, of the applicable chordal reference sheets. If you were dissatisfied with the sound of any chord shape (for example, a voicing with "A" as the top voice on the "E" string), go to the reference sheets, look down the column and try some of the other options in context. Also, try to use completely different voicings for an entire example. Finally, make up your own line with single notes and then carefully harmonize it as you would hear it. The choices you now make are sending you on your way to a concept that's all yours. No two players will make the same choices.

Example 51A: G minor 7

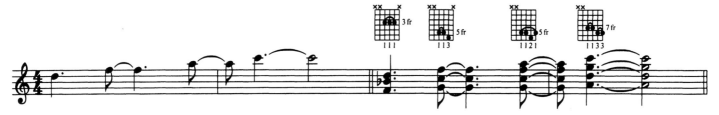

Example 51B

Example 51C

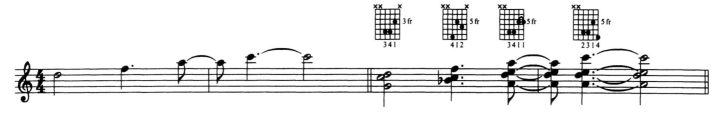

Example 51D

cadences:
approaches through
upper and lower neighbors

The notion of playing "outside" the harmonic boundaries has become an area of study for students of the music of Ornette Coleman, Miles Davis, John Coltrane, and all the supporting talents they've nurtured over the years.

Is there any agreed upon system of logic which applies to the tones, and configurations of pitches outside the "right notes?" I would like to offer my perspective on this, and it goes back to an old idea, that like good drama, good music must have tension and release. Without applying this notion and all its possibilities to harmony, we'd be left to create tension with only dynamics and velocity. It's my belief that virtually all passages which to our ears seem to be outside the acceptable concepts of harmony, can be explained as having some kind of "dominant function," (V7–I).

I'd like to offer the following exercise ideas as a means to explore this world through chordal movement. The essential idea is that you take a chord (where the top voice is a melody note) which has an emotional connection for you and try to surround it by using consonant (diatonic/within the chord scale or mode) and/or chromatic upper and lower neighbors to create a little tension as the harmony releases and comes to rest.

The given examples provide ideas for both major and minor tonics. If you see a note, especially a top voice which seems to make no sense in relation to the tonic, look back a bar or two and see if it is a part of the altered dominant (super locrian mode) scale of the V7 chord. In most cases, the answer should lie there, but, the real decision making factor will always be in PLAYING WHAT TRULY SOUNDS GOOD TO YOU!

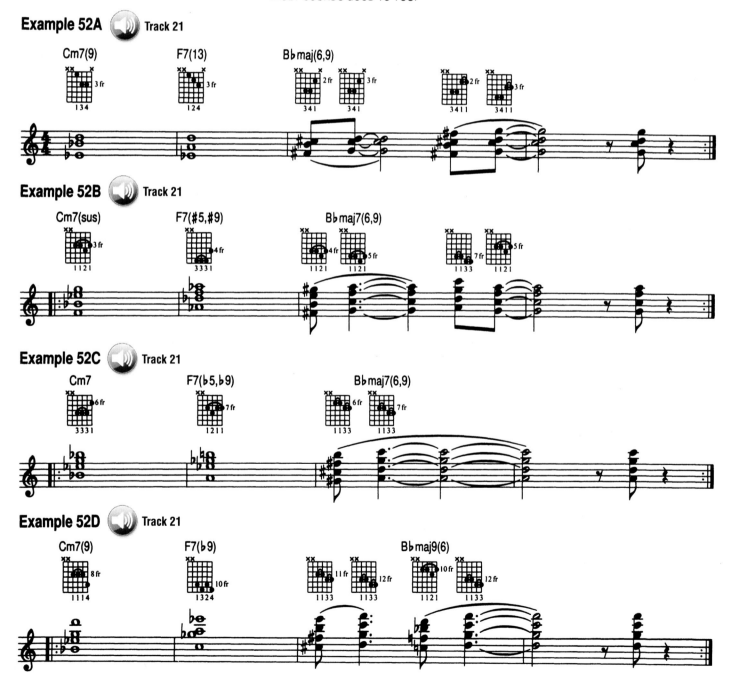

Example 52A — Track 21

Cm7(9)   F7(13)   Bbmaj(6,9)

Example 52B — Track 21

Cm7(sus)   F7(#5,#9)   Bbmaj7(6,9)

Example 52C — Track 21

Cm7   F7(b5,b9)   Bbmaj7(6,9)

Example 52D — Track 21

Cm7(9)   F7(b9)   Bbmaj9(6)

Steve Khan

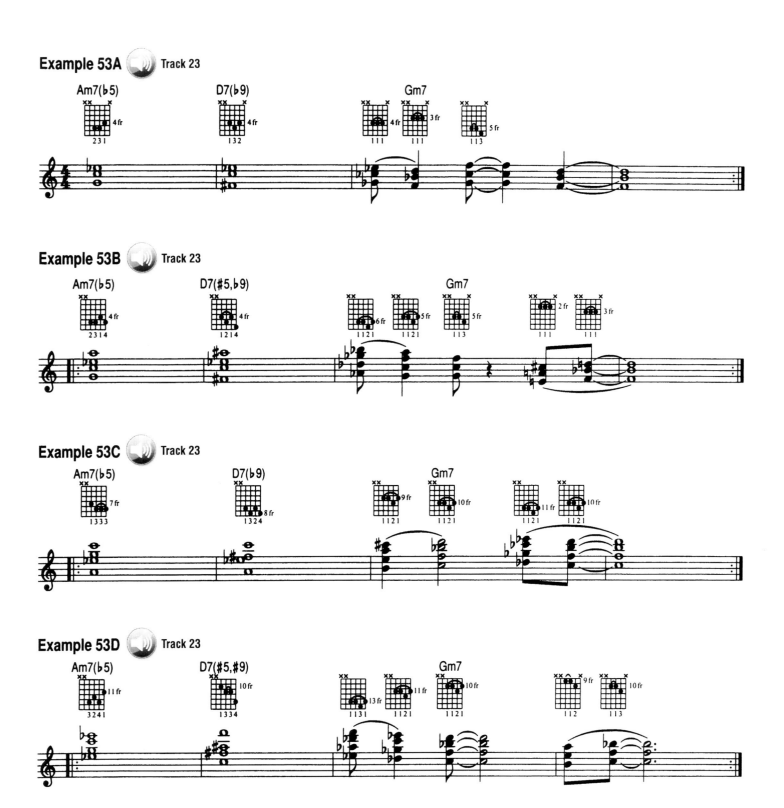

contemporary voicings reference

This series of chordal reference materials is, in essence, an extension of the previously presented unit titled MODES IN CHORDS. Again, the greater goal is to provide you with as many options as possible.

You'll notice that for this study, only two of the three basic chord families are represented: Major (lydian) and Minor (dorian). The dominant 7th (mixolydian) chord family has seemingly been omitted. This is really not so, and the thinking behind this is as follows: As has been stated and restated, as guitarists we can extend the harmony of any dominant 7th chord by superimposing iim7 voicings/chords over the V7 root. So, in this contemporary series of sound shapes we want to extend the harmony as often as possible. By only using minor (iim7) voicings against the V7 that's precisely what we would be accomplishing.

At times, the manner of this presentation of 4 and 3-note voicings/chords will seem very logical, and at other times, quite random. All in all, it's not a harmonically sequential reference. I've chosen this method to challenge your ears as well as your chordal dexterity so that, on a purely technical level, your fingers never get too comfortable at this stage. Like before, the melodic voice is found ascending on the high "E" or "B" string.

I believe the best exercise for initial and long term results is to play each voicing within a row, holding it for two bars over the "G" pedal on the recording. Establish your own feeling for what each sound-shape holds emotionally for you. As you begin to use the basic and contemporary voicings in conjunction with one another, your relationship to all that you hear and play will have a much deeper connection.

Try to create a series of short term practice goals and follow them through over a projected time frame. Always be patient with yourself and you'll find you're progressing almost without noticing it.

4-note open voicing systems

Example 54: G Lydian Mode

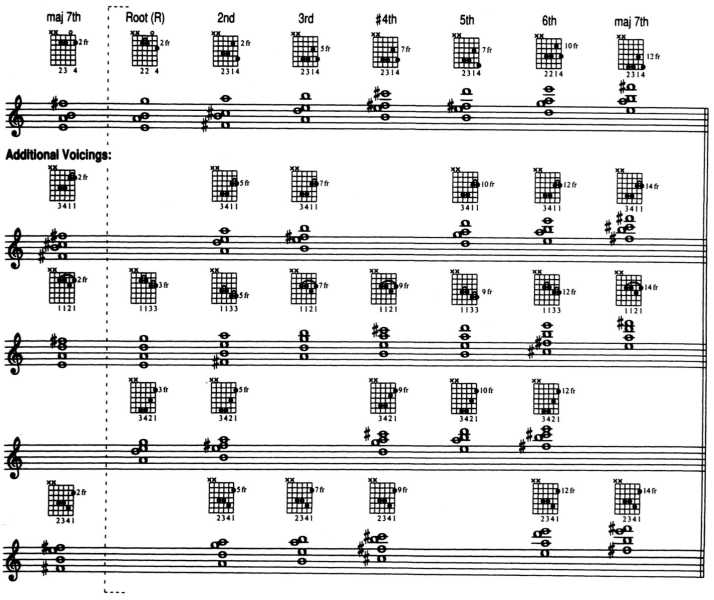

4-note open voicing systems

Example 55: G Dorian Mode

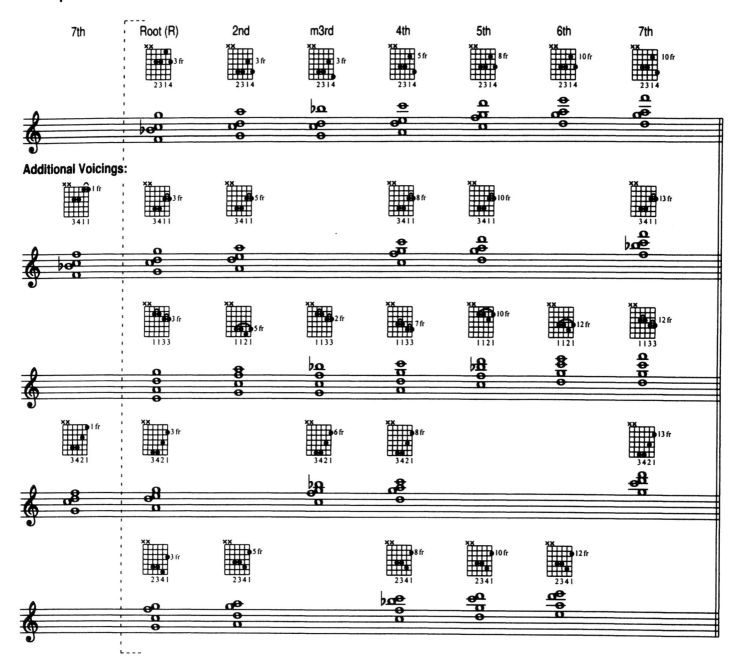

3-note open voicing systems

Example 56: G Lydian Mode

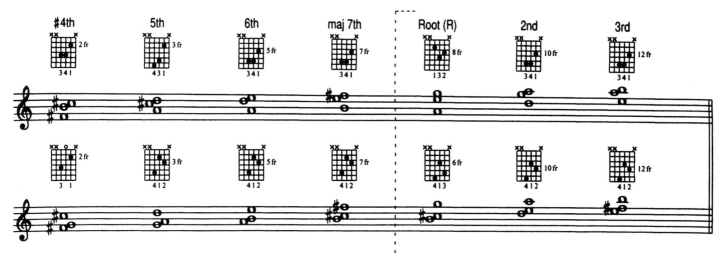

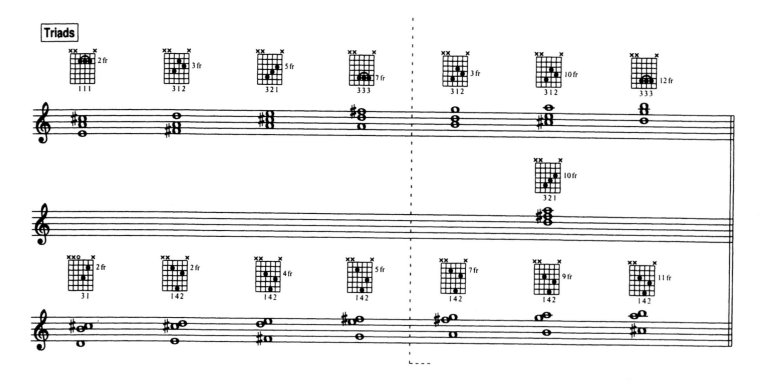

3-note open voicing systems

Example 57: G Dorian Mode

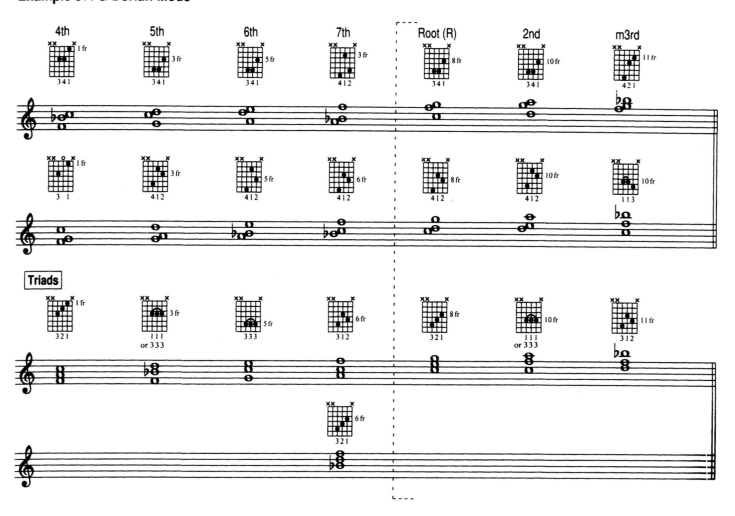

Steve Khan

additional voicing reference

Example 57A: G Lydian Mode

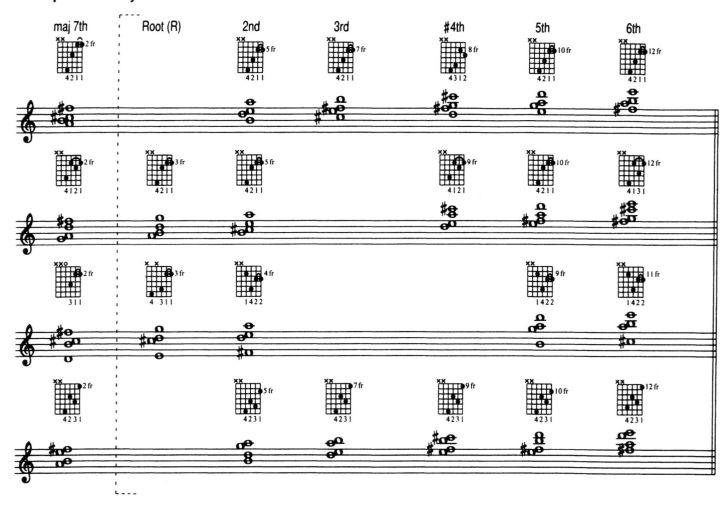

European Tour Poster, May, 1994. Left to right: Anthony Jackson, Steve, and Dennis Chambers.
Illustration: Ned Shaw

major/minor exercise

This is one of my personal favorite exercises! I'd like to present this one in an elongated study form. Let's analyze this repeated four-bar pattern as if it were a harmonic problem we needed to solve. In doing the work for you, as I might do it for myself, it's hoped that you'll be able to apply this same thought and analytical process when you have a problem with any series of chords within a song. The purpose is to expedite the process of HEARING THROUGH THE CHANGES as early as possible.

First, look at the chords and try and determine the chord family, and then the mode or scale based upon the root. In this case we have a Gmaj7 for 2 bars and a Gm7 for 2 bars. Generally speaking, in a jazz oriented context, when you come across a major chord, you use the lydian mode because, most times, the sound of the #4 is far more appealing to the ear than that of the natural 4th (the suspension). For most minor chords, you would apply the dorian mode.

For the next step, I would take the time to jot down the basic pentatonic possibilities using two simple formulas. On major chords, a player can apply minor pentatonics based upon the 3rd, 6th, and 7th degrees of the major scale. On any minor chord, a player may apply minor pentatonics (root, m3rd, 4th, 5th, and ♭7th) built upon the root, 2nd, and 5th; and, the dominant 7th pentatonic (Root, 2nd, 3rd, 5th, and ♭7th) built on the 4th degree of the dorian mode.

What's accomplished by just making this kind of effort is you've given yourself the chance to play through this chord progression and play the "right notes." Laying out the pentatonics gives you an initial opportunity to keep some of your lines closer to the blues language which is such a vital component in all popular music. But, in doing this, what's NOT accomplished, other than some basic improvising, is that you're not yet "speaking the language" of jazz or any other style, and, that's a discussion best left for another text.

For those of you who do want to improve your jazz playing and perhaps pursue a life in the music, how does this exercise work towards that goal? How many times have we seen progressions that look something like this:

Gmaj7 / Gm7 C7 / Fmaj7 / Fm7 B♭7 / E♭maj7 / E♭m7 A♭7 / D♭maj7 / Am7 D7

If we group the bars in two different ways, the functioning of the chords can take on two distinctly different looks. In one view, isolating bars 1–2; 3–4; 5–6; this movement could be seen as I-maj going to i-minor. You may be asking, how can you say that with (for example in bar 2) the C7 chord there? This is where the 2nd view comes into play. If we just look at bars 2–3(or 4–5; 6–7; and 8–1), Gm7, C7, and Fmaj7 are all in the key of F major. Gm7 (G dorian); C7 (C mixolydian); and Fmaj7 (F ionian) all have the same notes, just beginning and ending on different scale degrees. So, if we view bar 2 as only having Gm7 (G dorian) and choose not to observe the C7 because the pitches are the same, then bars 1–2 could be scene as moving from major to minor.

This exercise can be a preparation for negotiating such progressions in a diatonic manner. Again, the accomplishment of just hearing the "right" formations of sound through the chords paves the way for eventually adding the alterations (♭5, #5, ♭9, and #9) so that the tension created on the V7 chord resolves as you go to the I major tonic.

When trying to learn to hear the movement of harmony in order to improvise I firmly believe the most important first step is to "establish the chord sounds." I would always suggest beginning with the fundamental building blocks, your guide tones. Simple 2-note voicings which outline the harmony. I tend to associate these voicings as an integral part of Jim Hall's approach to accompaniment.

Example 58: Step 1 🔊 **Track 25**

Here we present the usage of long tones implying a melody in the top voice. You might start by playing a 3-note chord across the D–G–B strings followed by a 4-note chord adding a top voice on the "E" string. The idea is to make your top, higher voiced chord, function as a melodic "response" to the lower voiced chord. Here I've purposely used more traditional guitar voicings which we might associate with great players like Wes Montgomery, Kenny Burrell, Jim Hall, and Joe Pass.

Example 59: Step 2  Track 25

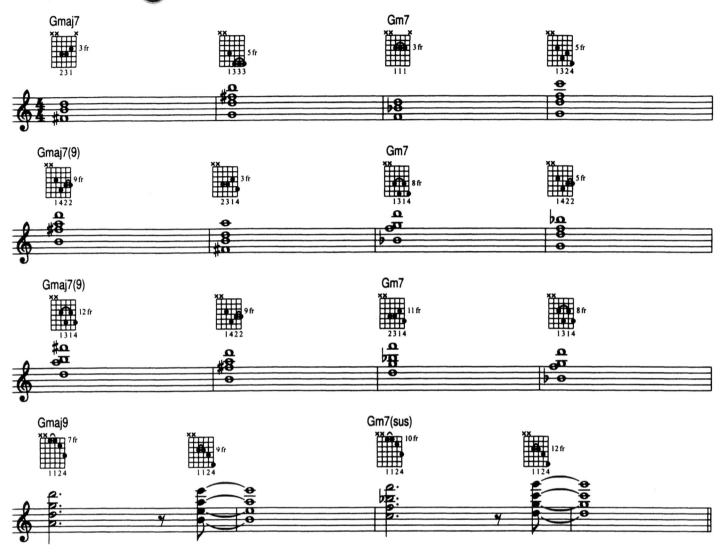

In this example you're presented with McCoy Tyner style voicings applied to the guitar. To condense the presentation, I've employed a "call and response" approach between the lower, 3-note voicings, and the higher register 4-note voicings. Usage of this style should give you a more modern and open sound.

Example 60: Step 3 🔊 **Track 25**

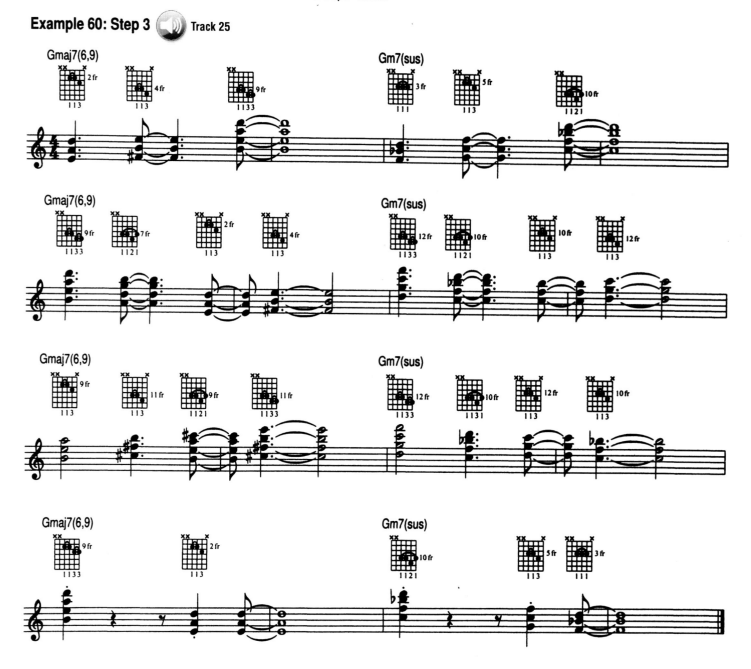

Steve Khan

This step is devoted entirely to 3-note voicings offering a healthy cross between closed-style chords, which one might associate with Bill Evans (bars 9–12), and open-style chords associated with players like McCoy Tyner, Herbie Hancock, Chick Corea, Joe Zawinul, and Keith Jarrett. These chord color tones from the extended harmony do wonders to open-up the texture for you and for the soloist you might be supporting.

Example 61: Step 4 Track 25

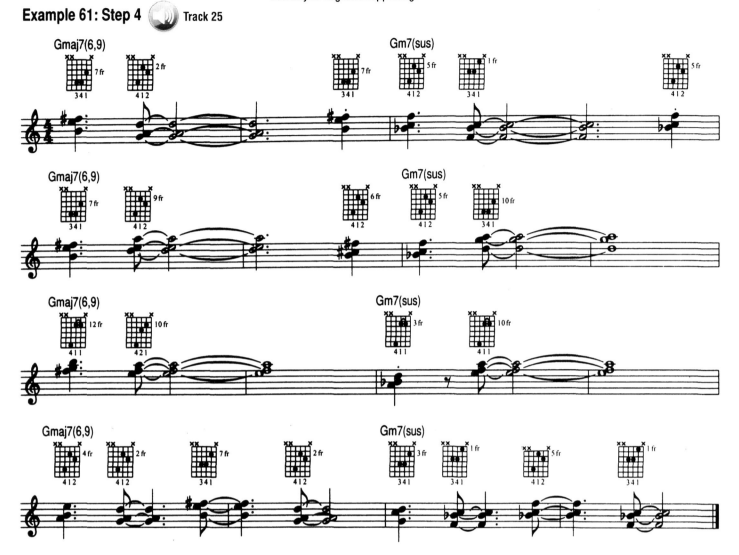

In this final presentation, we're using larger open-voicings with an ascending melodic top voice. It's presented using long tones to force you to GO SLOWLY and hear the content of each chord shape over the root. In doing this, you're developing a personal attachment to each sound. Before playing any chord, make certain that each note is speaking properly — that no one string is accidentally being muted or muffled.

As you know, you can use the CONTEMPORARY VOICINGS REFERENCE SHEETS which were laid out precisely for this exercise. They're in place to make sure that these options are right in front of you and made easy to explore. When learning how to hear these sounds as part of your approach, try to keep the movement of your top voice down to a whole note or half note as the harmonic movement will still be clear.

Example 62: Step 5 Track 25

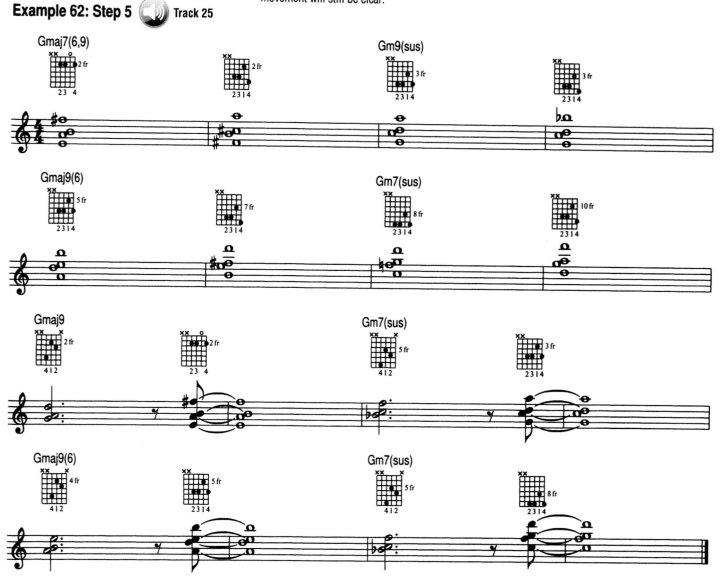

chord changes
for standards

One could certainly spend volumes presenting "standard" chordal movements/progressions from popular song forms (A–A–B–A and A–A') but, I chose to use just two examples which would lend themselves as exercises for this material. Both tunes present harmonic movements which are constant and very logical.

Example 63 ("Mundo Desmondo") is performed with a bossa nova feeling which, as an even 8th-note groove, can be close to jazz and Latin jazz, as well as lighter forms of Pop, Rock, and R&B. You're given a basic rhythm along with the essential bass notes leaving your chordal choices to speak clearly. In this first example, you're asked to explore the usage of both inversions of the guide tones. As you're allowed to mark the chord changes without any keyboard interference, you should hear just how clearly these two-note guide tones outline the harmonic movement.

Example 64 offers comping in an orchestral style. The idea is that, with your guitar, you have a big band in your hands. The concept being, that you imagine the top note of the chord voicings (on the "B" string) as the saxophone or trombone section, and the 3- or 4-note voicings with the top note on the "E" string as the trumpets. Dynamics are important here, and you might try playing the lower voiced chords at mezzo piano and the high-voiced chords at forte.

Letter B, of Example 64, is an example of using octave leaps in your top voice. Remember it's a melodic voice and an octave can be a very expressive interval. A simple suggestion, try this movement in reverse.

The final section (A3) presents the concept of having the top voice slowly ascending through the progression. In your own improvising, try, once again, to reverse the process creating one long descending line in your top voice throughout the progression.

Example 65 offers my own approach based upon a Tyner-influenced guitar style. If you've familiarized yourself with the presentation of how to actualize his voicings on the guitar then this example should make a lot of sense. I'd like to point out one special harmonic approach which I associate with McCoy Tyner and you can observe and listen to this as you play at A2, bars 2 and 4; B, bar 5; and A3, bar 6. What he does so often over a iim7–V7 is to immediately play the 13th-type chord voicing of the V7 even though the bassist usually observes the roots of both the iim7 and the V7. You might have to force yourself to make use of this approach, as opposed to always playing a iim7 chord voicing first, but, if you find an emotional connection to the sound, then you will in time strike a balance with its usage.

Example 66A ("Some Things You're Not") begins with the guide tone approach. It is my firm belief that this is always a good place to start and then expand your concept from there. One little "trick" to take note of (in bars 3, 11, 18, 22, 27, and 34) is that over a V7 chord I often use the guide tones from the previous iim7 for the first two beats, giving the sound a heightened feeling of suspension and release. Try playing these bars with only the dominant 7th guide tones and listen to the difference, then, make your own choices.

Example 66B employs a McCoy Tyner/Chick Corea approach for the entire tune. It should be noted that if you were to attempt to play exactly like this behind the melody or a soloist you would be guilty of some serious overplaying. For the purposes of this book I've tried to jam in as much information as possible, but, in a real playing context you would have to weed out a lot of this while listening to what's going on around you.

I'm often asked to apply some of the "Open Voicing" concepts to a standard. In Example 66C I took one chordal "sound shape" from the "Open Voicings" reference pages and attempted to apply it to every bar if possible. As this example stands, it is a composite of the open voicing concept and the Tyner/Corea approach and should add to your growing sense that these voicings are becoming popular sound shapes—things you really hear.

Since all the play-along examples were constructed with the aid of computer sequencers, I have chosen to use an R&B oriented shuffle feel, with some Latin undertones, as a substitute for a jazz-like medium bounce. To my ear it's still difficult to make machines feel like Elvin Jones, Roy Haynes, Jack DeJohnette, Al Foster, Tony Williams or Philly Joe Jones. It's also my feeling that the shuffle is a feel, an attitude, that most musicians, from all genres, can relate to.

Example 63: "Mundo Desmondo" (Guide Tones) Track 27

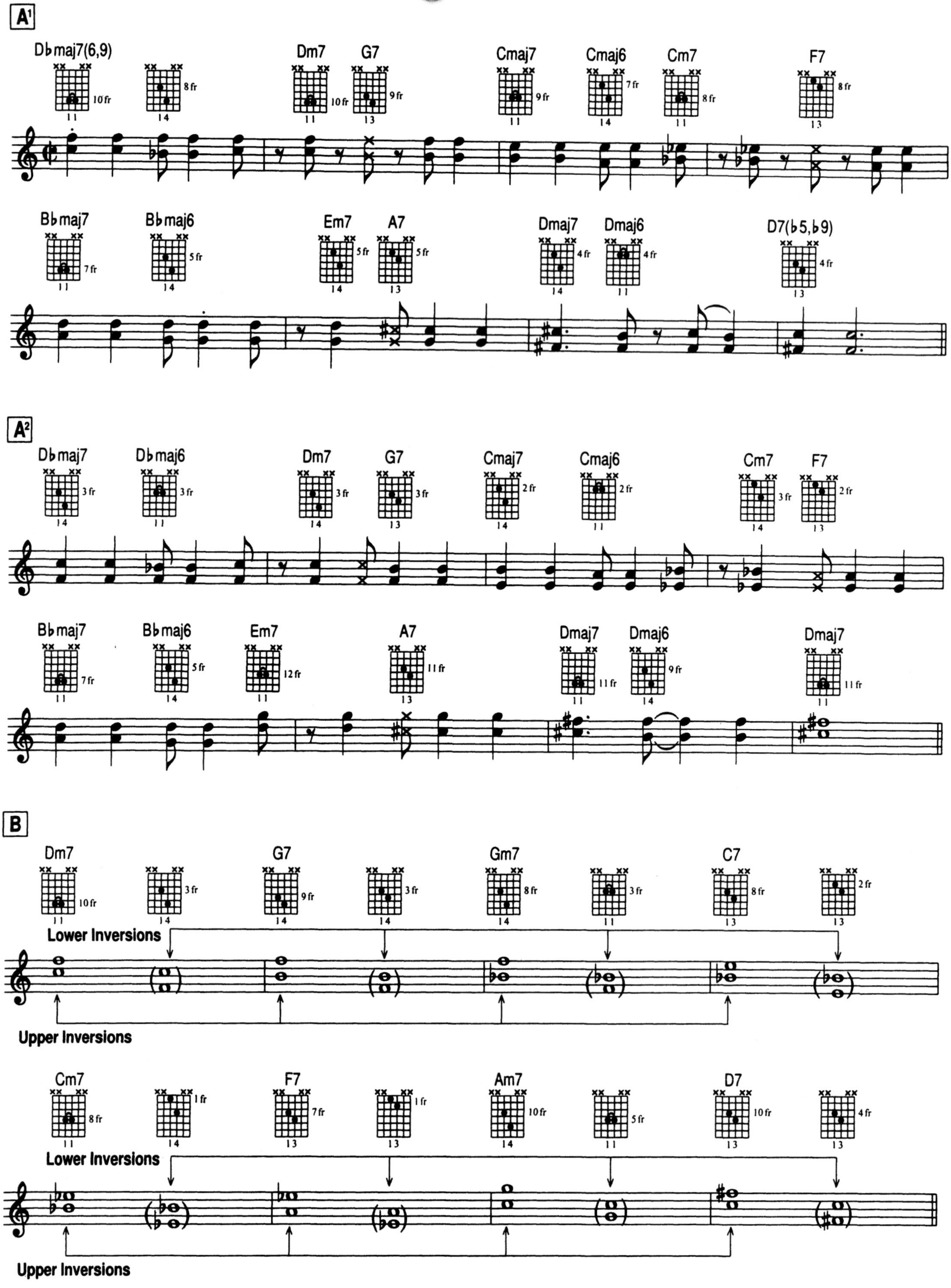

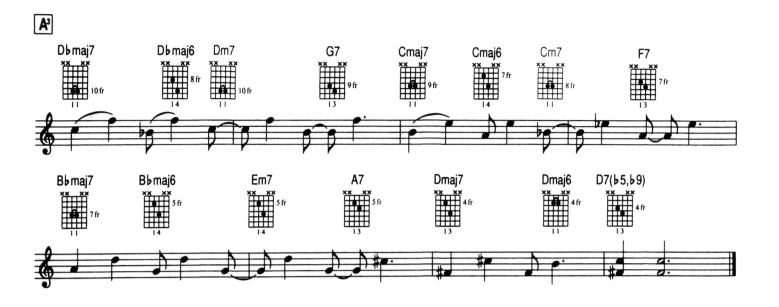

Example 64: Orchestral-Style Comping Track 27

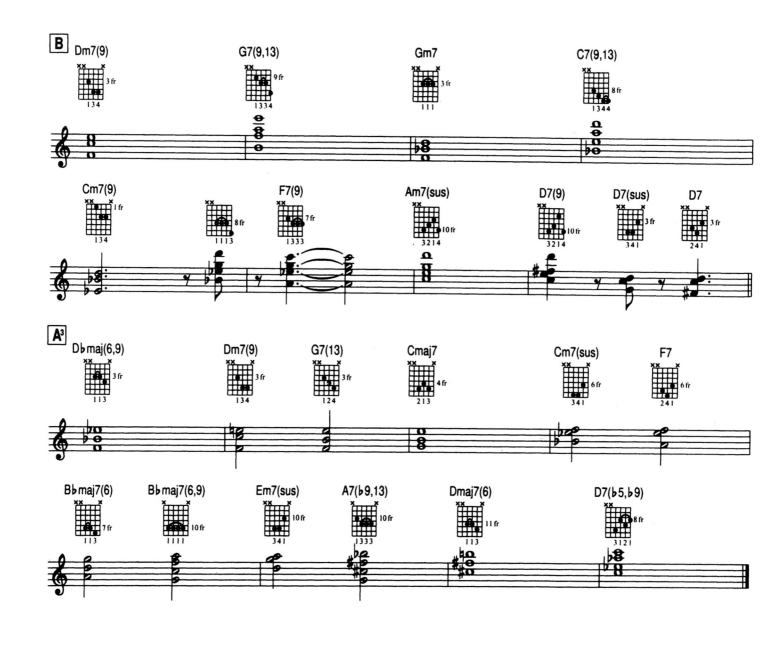

Example 65: Contemporary-Style Comping Track 27

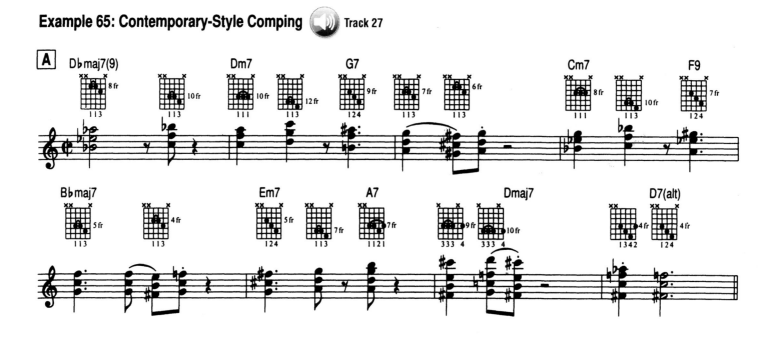

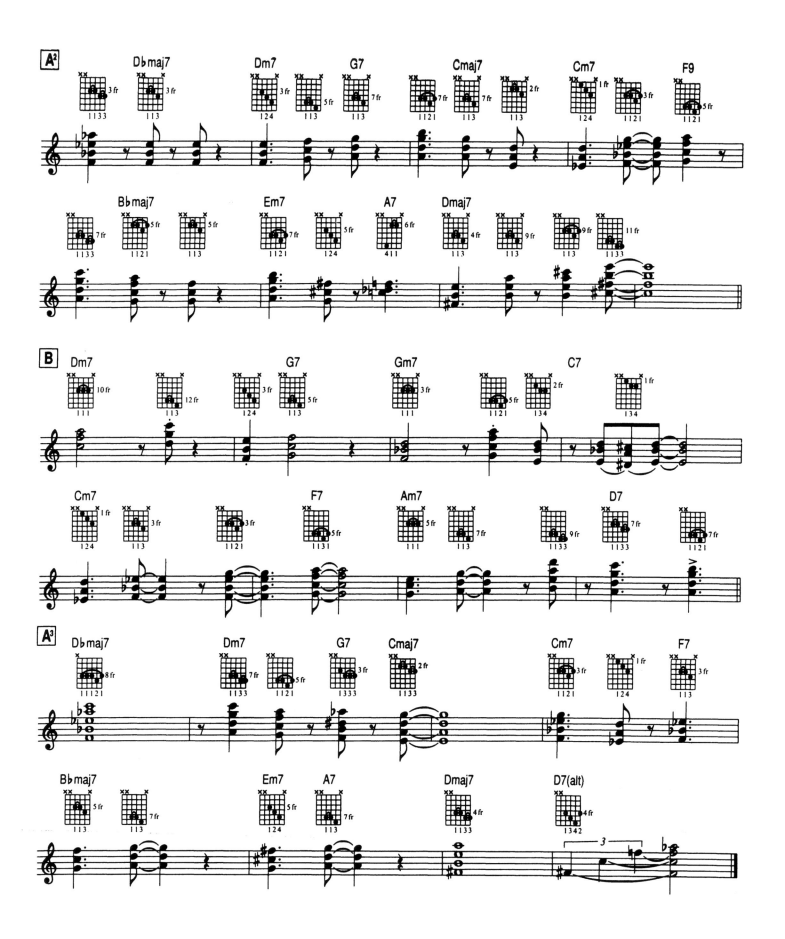

Example 66B: Contemporary Style Track 29

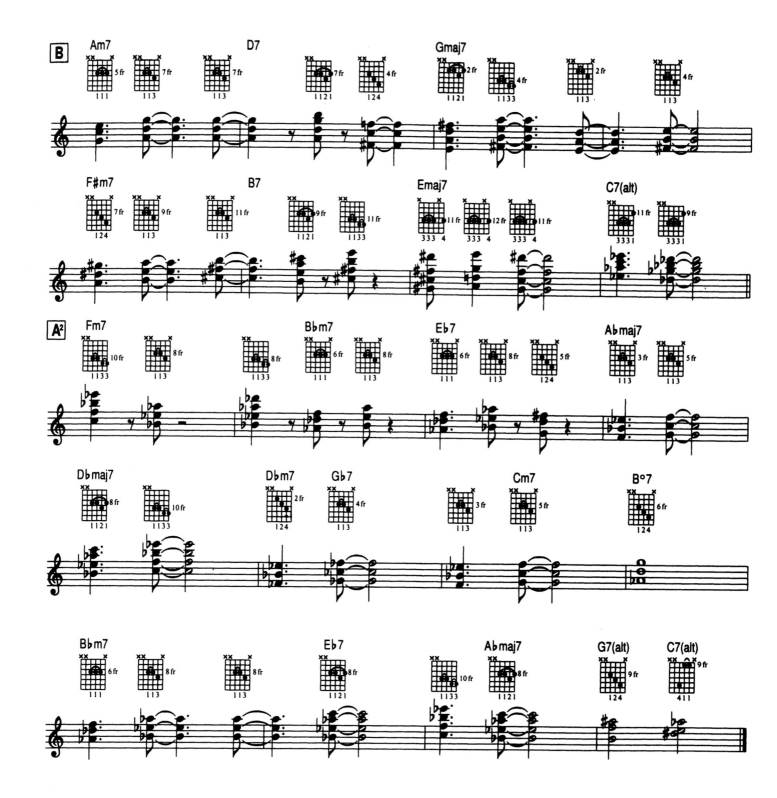

Steve Khan

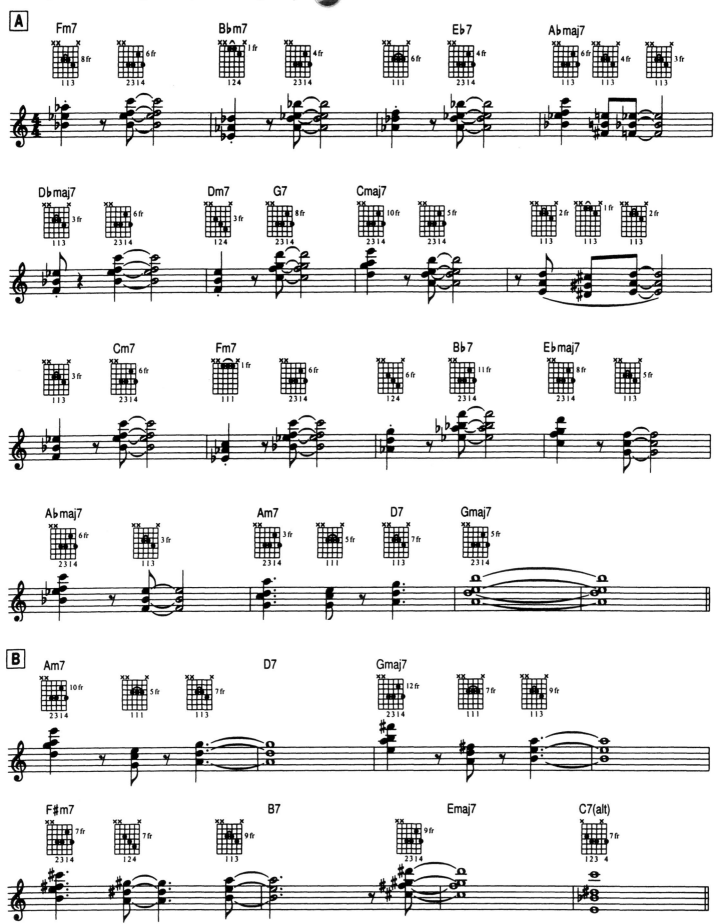

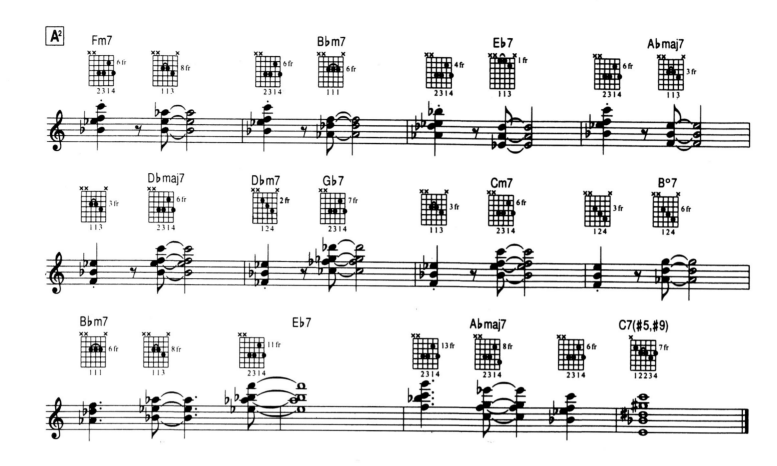

Publicity photo taken by Aldo Mauro in the basement of my apartment
in the Chelsea section of Manhattan, 1988

Steve Khan

Gm7-E♭maj7(♯4)

It's the continuing goal of this book to inspire you to come up with your own simple practice exercises and devices which would accelerate the process of "hearing through the changes." The following is one of my favorites, because for the most part, many of the voicings can sustain themselves through both chords though these two chords might seem unrelated.

Again the movement between the chords is simple and repetitive, a four-bar phrase, two bars for each chord. So why would these chords have so much in common? Let's look at the modal pitches first:

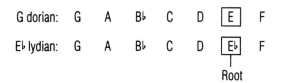

As you can see, though G dorian is derived from the key of F major and E♭ lydian the key of B♭ major, they only differ over the usage of E♮ or E♭. So, to put it simply, as long as you avoid those pitches, any chord voicing you play will sustain through the entire four bars.

Example 67 focuses on long tones. The chords stay the same and only the bass note moves. Yet, the change is made and will actually sound obvious. Example 67B features inner-voice motion while the top-voice remains fixed. Try playing these as written, in broken chords, or in an arpeggiated style and of course use your own rhythmic ideas.

Example 68 contains some vamp ideas utilizing triads in conjunction with 3-note open voicings. The short focus is on common-note top voices with the motion in the inner-voices. You should discover while playing and listening to these vamps just how contemporary simple triads can sound when used alongside voicings which might be considered modern.

Example 69 features a stationary top and bottom voice with only the middle moving back and forth between "A" and "C." In bars 8, 12, and 16, I've added a kind of chordal answer to the phrase, again beginning with 2-note voicings and building to 4 notes.

Example 67A (with Common Tone Top Voice) Track 31

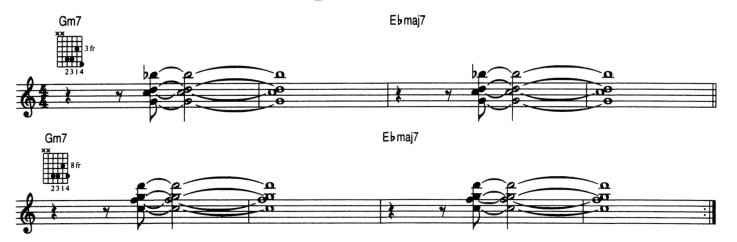

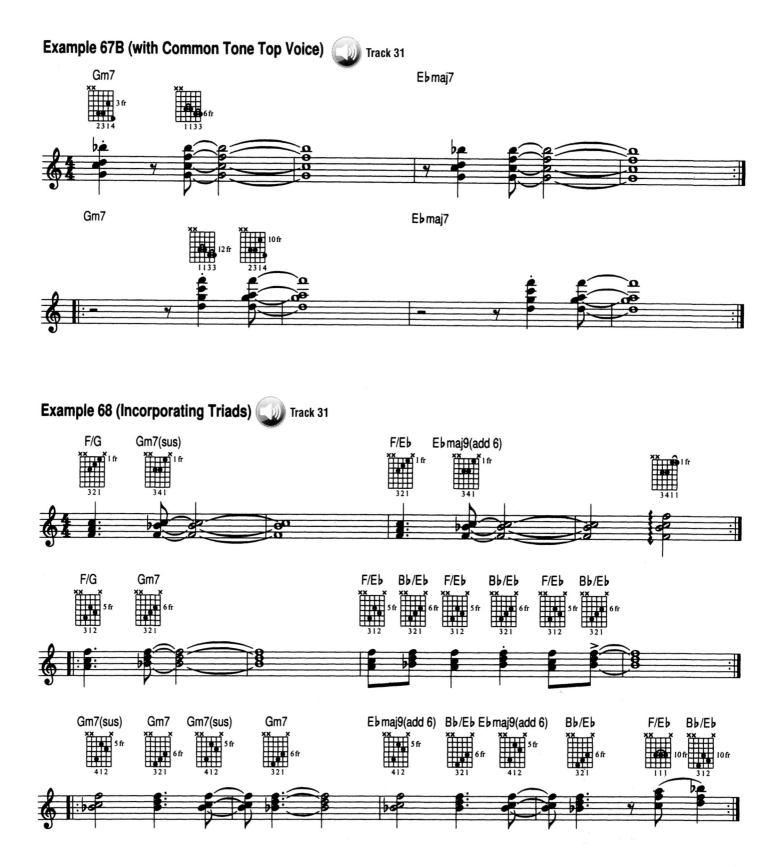

Example 68 (Incorporating Triads) Track 31

Example 69 (with Inner Voice Movement)  Track 31

Weather Update European Tour, Perugia, Italy, July 13, 1986.
Left to right: Joe Zawinul, Peter Erskine, Victor Bailey, Steve, and Robert Thomas, Jr. Photo: Carlo Pieroni

octaves with thirds inside

In attempting to cover as much material as possible, I also want to present an option which may barely qualify as a "chord," but can certainly give us more sonic variety. For students of guitar history, I'd have to say that, in this area, George Benson has done the deepest exploration through improvising with these formations.

The form is that of an octave played across the "A" and "B" strings or the "D" and high "E" strings with the interval of a 3rd added on the "G" string in the former, and the "B" string in the latter. Just try and conceive of these forms as just another sound shape, another means of coloring a melodic pitch. It's additional material to the chordal fundamentals and extensions presented in the "reference" series of materials. A simple practice suggestion: try and apply these chordal shapes within any of the exercises and examples presented in the book. Select an exercise/example use the top voice as your point of reference and then substitute the corresponding octave plus 3rd from the same chord family and see how it sounds.

Example 70A: G Dorian

Top Voice on "E" String

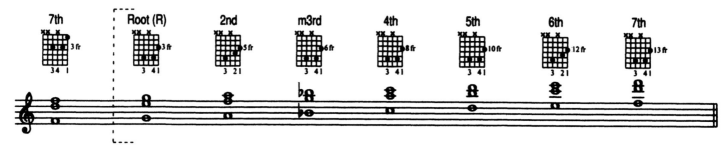

Top Voice on "B" String

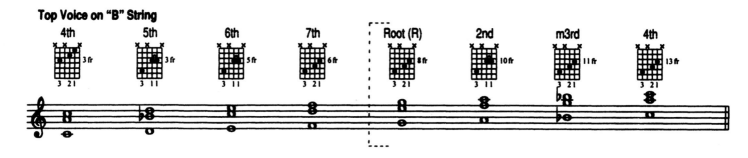

Example 70B: G Lydian

Top Voice on "E" String

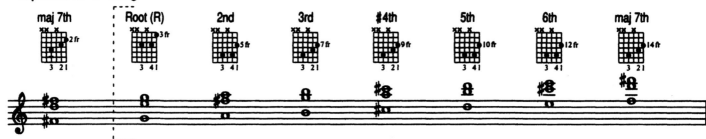

Top Voice on "B" String

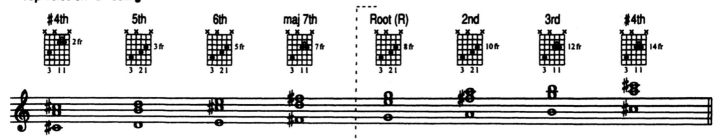

Example 70C: G Mixolydian

Top Voice on "E" String

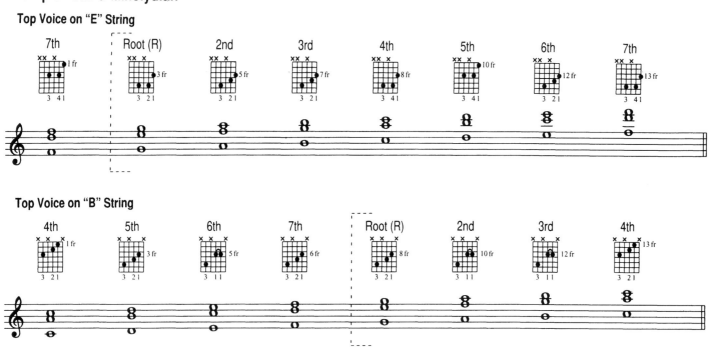

Top Voice on "B" String

With the Brecker Bros. Band at the Village Gate on July 21, 1975.
From left to right: David Sanborn, Michael Brecker, Randy Brecker, and Steve. Photo: Erika Price

C7 pedal chordal reference

Often in a solo section or just a long jam over a vamp, you're asked to play over a static dominant 7th chord. For years of private teaching, and at clinics and seminars I've been asked by players how they can expand what they can do over these kinds of situations. The following reference charts are offered as a basis to work from.

Begin with the basic notion of establishing the sound of the dominant 7th chord, in this case C7. Generally speaking, these voicings will contain "E" naturals and "B" flats somewhere within. Often you can extend the harmony beyond these sounds by adding iim7 voicings usually associated with Gm7 chords. In doing this you're essentially replacing those "E" naturals with "F"s so that almost all the chords have a suspended feeling.

As with all our other chordal reference charts this one is to serve as a place to return to when you're held back by a particular problem. Perhaps the answer will lie within the following examples.

Example 71: Mixolydian (Basic Voicings)

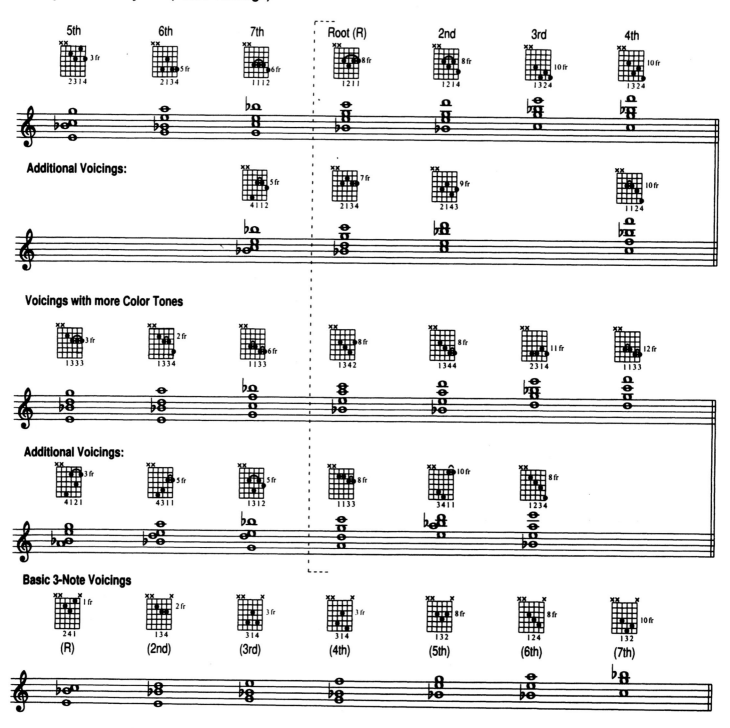

Example 72: Dorian (Basic Voicings)

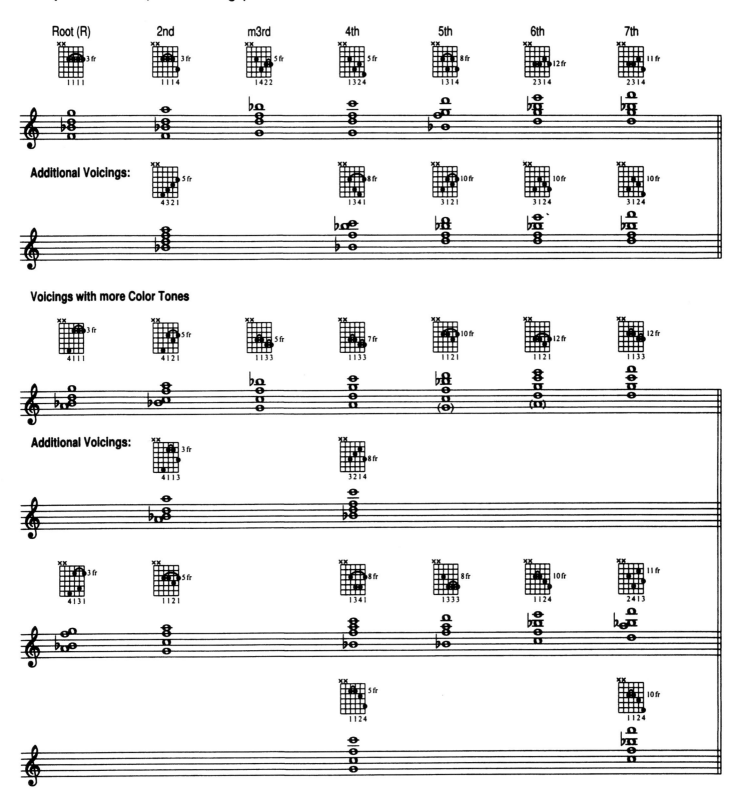

Example 73: G Dorian 4-Note Open Voicings (Mode Ascends on "E" String)

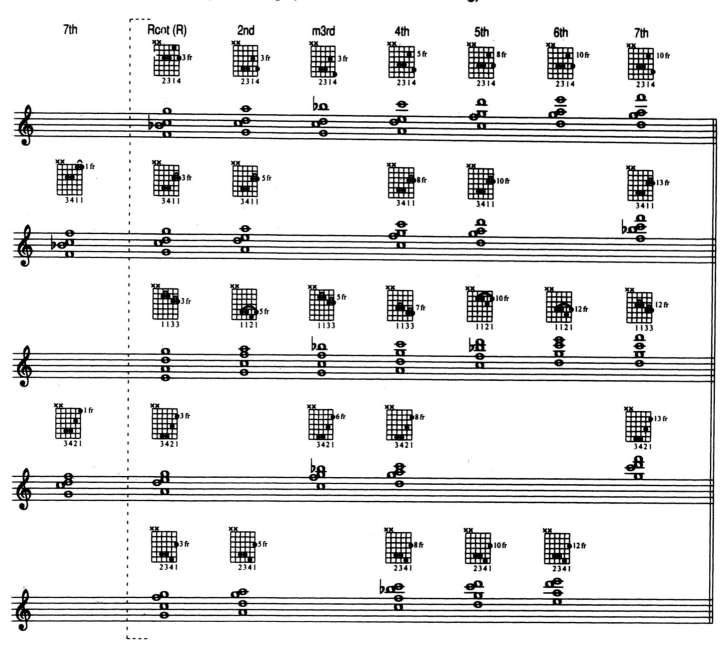

Example 74: G Dorian 3-Note Voicings (Mode Ascends on "B" String)

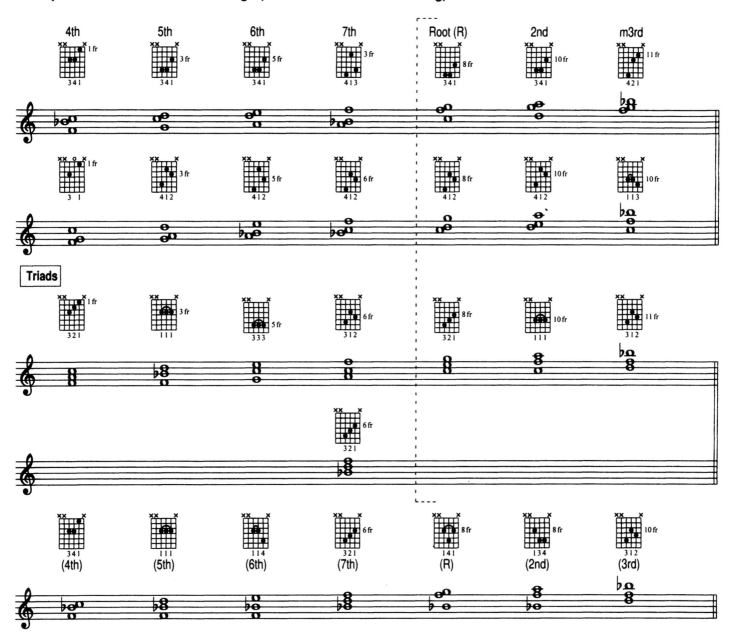

about the recording

Probably the most difficult aspect of this endeavor, and for that matter, teaching or giving a clinic to a large group, is to make the work inspiring and educational for those who have the farthest to go without sounding like you are talking down to the more advanced players. It's an extremely fine line to walk and doubtlessly, somewhere along the way, someone feels slighted. I am now hoping that for most of you I've walked that fine line in an acceptable manner.

The examples which are presented on the recording were done at tempos designed to offer CLARITY; so that you can hear what I am doing and then practice the same thing without it being too difficult. Generally speaking the performed examples on the recording will be followed by the same track, only minus my guitar, leaving the now empty space to be filled by you. There will be cases however, such as the G blues examples and various pedals, where you are offered several different 'feels' or 'grooves' with which to experiment using the same written examples.

In Examples 20–31 where the written music is offered in whole-notes and half-notes, you are free to play them in precisely that manner, but, I've also suggested that you try to work on your own 'feel' by improvising simple rhythms. This is what I did in performing those examples. If you like what I did, sometimes it can be a great learning exercise to transcribe the rhythms I played. The pitches will be just as they appear.

In Examples 33–36, once again you will see that the exercise was presented in whole-notes. Initially it is important to practice them in that manner and make certain that each voice is speaking. Another method which can accomplish the same end is to play the chords in a 'broken chord' style. In the performance of these examples, you will hear, at times, that this is what I did. Please try doing it this way as well.

Though engineer Malcolm Pollack and I have done our best to share with you the technical details of most of the sounds you will hear on the audio presentations not everything turned out exactly as I had hoped. On a number of the recorded examples, you will hear some distortion on the guitar sound. Do not worry!!! It is not your audio, it is not your stereo. It was actually my fault. At the time of the recording I didn't understand one of the controls on the amp and did not fully realize exactly what kind of sound was going to tape until we went to mix it. So, to all of you, my apologies. The lesson here is to ALWAYS take the extra time to double-check such things. It will save you great embarrassment later!

From the moment it was known there would be a play-along recording included with the book, I planned on including several improvised pieces. Pieces which would not necessarily exist as fully realized compositions but would serve to demonstrate just how your lines and chordal harmony can be presented side-by-side while you're actually playing. It is hoped that the pieces will inspire each of you to work hard at putting to use concepts from the book in your own music, but, IN YOUR OWN WAY!!! I would like to say a little about each of the pieces.

"Don Grolnelius" **Track 33**

Over the course of the book, reflections on the influence of pianists on my work was a constant. There exists, up until this moment, the absence of one very significant pianist and person in my life, Don Grolnick. Though Don passed away earlier this year (1996), his influence on me personally and musically can be felt throughout. During the earliest of our days with the Brecker Bros. Band, we used to rehearse/jam in Don's apartment in the Village in New York City. Incredibly, Don lived in a building where his neighbors were Will Lee and Chris Parker . . . so, the whole rhythm section was right there, in residence! During the early '70s, we were all SOUL TRAIN fans and Don worked really hard at perfecting his Don Cornelius impression. If you can picture Don Grolnick's persona and stature, it's a pretty big stretch for him to get this impression down . . . but, he worked and worked at mastering the "Love, Peace, and Soul!" good-bye from the show. Finally, one day he got pretty close to it and Will called him Don Grolnelius. Anyway, I wanted to improvise one example pulling together all that is suggested in Unit 19. I decided to use our basic shuffle groove (itself a tribute to drummer Bernard Purdie) and try and evoke a sense of Don's immense keyboard presence. Having spent so many years making music with him, his influence on how I play, and now stand as my own hodgepodge of styles — perhaps mostly a mix of R&B, Jazz, and Latin — is, in part, due to Don. We all loved him, his music, and being his friends. We miss him deeply.

"Sliceville"  **Track 37**

On Don's last CD, "MEDIANOCHE" (Warner Bros.), he explored Latin jazz. Don's composition, "Rainsville," essentially a sophisticated blues with a cha-cha feel, was my favorite tune without question. I simply extracted the Bb key, the attitude, and just kind of put my own spin on it. As our hasty mixes went, I have to say that I now feel the guitar sound here is as close as I've gotten to sounding as I'd like. Odd, in this context, because I remember Don really disliking reverb to the degree I like to employ it. The title is a nod to Don's tune . . . also in our own slang . . . when you've been fired, or things don't work out, well, you've been "sliced" and you're on the last train to "Sliceville."

"Khalatmo"  Track 39

This is actually the title of my play-along Latin file in Al Gorgoni's computer system, now Mac's Studio Vision. It sounded so funny, I decided to use it as a title. The chord progression is inspired by one of the tunes on Cal Tjader's "SOUL BURST" LP from the mid-'60s which features some brilliant Chick Corea piano work . . . work which changed my whole approach to playing! It's an 8-bar vamp:

¢ ‖: F7 / F7 / B♭7 / B♭7 / B♭7 / B♭7 / F7 / F7 :‖

It's a great dominant 7th workout, terrific for employing the superimposition of iim7 chords.

"Gracinha" Track 41

This piece is simply an 8 bar, double-time, Bb turnaround:

¢ ‖: Cm7 / Cm7 / F7 / F7(alt.) / B♭maj /╱./ ╱./ G7(alt.) :‖

Though it has little to do with Brasilian music, it is named for Gracinha Laporace-Mendes, the most incredible vocalist, and wife of pianist/arranger, Sergio Mendes. His last two CDs, "BRASILEIRO" and "OCEANS," have been in my CD trays constantly. In Grancinha's voice and phrasing is everything that makes music so uplifting and inspiring. For guitarists, these CDs feature the brilliant accompaniment of Paul Jackson, Jr., also easily worth the price of admission. He sounds fantastic on these recordings!!!

"Cintura City" Track 35

After spending so much of the last couple of years hanging out and hearing all the great Salsa vocalists and their bands in the clubs of Manhattan, Brooklyn, Queens, and the Bronx, plus taking Salsa/Mambo dance lessons, I now understand why so many lyrics pay tribute to the movement of the waists (la cintura) of women dancing. As I grew-up in Los Angeles, specifically Westwood, when I was a little kid a new business area was being built-up, Century City . . . so, I guess this is sort of a play on words . . . VERY sort of!!!! This is also a simple vamp, 4 bars repeated:

¢ ‖: A♭7 / A♭7 / B♭m7 / B♭m7 :‖

The chord progression and feel is kind of a hybrid of two influences: (1) The Puerto Rico All-Stars' CD, "De Regresso" and (2) "Africando" Vol. 2. This track offers the exchange of two different guitar sounds: (1) my regular sound presenting only the chords for 16 bars; and (2) one of my overdrive sounds employing the Ibanez Tube Screamer for 16 bars of lines. For those lines, I used a '335' tone setting which Carlos Rios showed me years ago. Here it is: Put your pick-up selector in the middle position so both pick-ups are on. Then have the bridge pick-up set with the Volume control on '10' and the Tone control on '8'-'10'. The "trick" is that your neck pick-up only uses the Volume control at '5', keeping its Tone control at about '8'. When playing live, and for 99% of the playing heard here and on my CDs, I only use the neck pick-up with the tone control as low as '5' sometimes . . . When recording this drives engineers nuts!!! Both, Malcolm Pollack and James Farber beg me to "brighten-up" some . . . So I go to about '8' . . . Now, back to the Ibanez Tube Screamer, it has three controls and they are set as follows: LEVEL: 11 O'clock; DRIVE: 12 O'clock; and the final control setting is the key . . . TONE: shut-off!!! In addition to this, I do NOT use the chorus pedal at all with this sound! I have not used a sound like this on ANY CD of mine since '79 . . . and I don't think my sound then was half this good. These days the only time I even fool around with this sound is at clinics and during sound checks. I hope you all enjoy it.

Main Guitar: Gibson ES–335 (from the 1980s Heritage Series)
2nd Guitar: Fender Stratocaster (ca. 1963) with EMG pick-ups;
                       DiMarzio Bridge with Gibson Spacing
                       NOTE: used only on E♭ Triad Example 7
Amplifier: Walter Woods Stereo Preamp/Power Amp
Speakers: Two Marshall '1912' Speakers — each cabinet with one 12" speaker (Stock)
Effects: Ernie Ball Volume Pedal, Ibanez EBL-5 Effects Pedal Board

Pedal Board contains five pedals, 99% of the time, I only use three of them. The main source of 'my' sound is the Ibanez DCF-10 Chorus/Flanger Pedal (Metallic Blue in color). The specific settings are as follows:

MODE DIAL: Position [3] (4–32 m/sec.)
DELAY TIME: 11 o'clock
SPEED: 12 o'clock
WIDTH: 2 o'clock
DELAY LEVEL: 2 o'clock
REGENERATION: Shut-off

There are two digital delay pedals in the board. Harry Kolbe (Amp and Electronics Genius) wired up the pedal board with a 'micro-mixer' so that the two delays go out LEFT & RIGHT. They have a random setting . . . one side at a quarter note (IF I'm really being careful!!!), and the other side with a quarter note triplet. For recording they're set to put out at VERY low levels or Malcolm will kill me!!!

SOUND CONCEPT: What I'm TRYING to achieve with this sound is to have the single notes SOUND as if they are unchorused, but, when a voicing is played, the chorusing should 'open-up' and exist as a huge sound of beauty. At times, I'm hoping it sounds like Larry Young's incredible organ sound . . . even though I know it's not even close!!! To this day, I have not found one single other pedal which gets me any closer to this sound!

All of the instruments other than Steve's guitar were mixed "live" as they emerged from Al Gorgoni's sequencing equipment, the guitar being the only thing that required something as old-fashioned as a tape recorder. In this case, the tape machine was an Otari 1" 16-track, model MX-70, and the console was a TAC Scorpion.

The guitar was recorded with a pair of Neumann u87s, one in front of each cabinet. The microphones were a foot or so from the grillecloth, and slightly off the main speaker axis, using a cardioid pattern, no low-end roll off, and with the internal 10 dB pads switched on. The signal was sent to tape unequalized, but slightly compressed. The compressor used was a dbx 166 stereo compressor (as can be found, I believe in every project studio in existence), set at a modest 2:1 ratio. I imagine the gain reduction rarely exceeded 3 dB, although I can't be sure of that, as I certainly didn't spend much of the session watching it.

The mixing was done with a very basic setup — two reverbs, a delay, and a stereo pitch-shifter, as follows:

Yamaha Rev-5: Vocal Plate. The only things I usually edit in this preset are the diffusion, which I like at 10 instead of the usual 5, and the E.R./Reverb parameter (one of the "internal parameters"), which I set to 20%. A nice transparent reverb.

Lexicon PCM-70: Rich Chamber. Rather denser, and darker, than any of the Yamaha reverb algorithms. I customarily edit this preset rather extensively. Here are the new settings of the parameters I changed:

Location	Parameter	Value
[0.6]	High Cutoff	9.02 kHz
[1.0]	RT Low (Reverb Time)	2.05 s
[1.1]	RT Mid	1.25 s
[1.3]	RT High Cutoff	5.75 kHz
[2.0]	Diffusion	99

Yamaha SPX-90: Pitch Change C. A simple stereo harmonizer algorithm, without any edits. I used it mostly to treat the delay, but also used just a little of it on the guitar.

Yamaha SPX-90: Delay L,R. A delay. This program offers a stereo output, but I only used one side. I *didn't* edit anything here, except of course the delay time, which varied from piece to piece depending on the tempo and the feel. Usually it was set at an interval corresponding to an eighth-note, a dotted eighth-note, or a quarter-note triplet, and generally was in the 200-to-350 millisecond range. I am tempted to digress at length about delay, which can be used in many subtle ways to add life and depth to mixes. However, as this is Steve's book and not mine, I shall refrain. In this case, the delayed signal, after a bit of high-end roll-off and some feedback, was not added directly to the mix, but instead was sent only to the pitch-shifter.

–Malcolm Pollack
Brooklyn, NY

Steve Khan Discography

These recordings feature:
Randy Brecker, Michael Brecker, David Sanborn, Don Grolnick, Will Lee, Mike Mainieri, and Steve Gadd:

"Tightrope"	Columbia, JC 34857	1977
"The Blue Man"	Columbia, JC 35539	1978
"Arrows"	Columbia, JC 36129	1979
"The Best of Steve Khan"	Columbia, JC 36406	1980
"The Collection"	Columbia, CK 57907	1994

Solo acoustic guitar:

"Evidence"	Arista/Novus, AN/3023	1981
	RCA/Novus, 3074-2-N	1990
	Polydor, POCJ-1892 [Japan]	

Steve Khan and Eyewitness recordings featuring Anthony Jackson, Steve Jordan, and Manolo Badrena:

"Eyewitness"	Antilles, 422-848-821	1981
	Polydor, POCJ-1893 [Japan]	
"Blades"	Passport Jazz, PJ 88001	1982
As "Modern Times"	Polydor, POCJ-1894 [Japan]	
"Casa Loco"	Antilles, 422-848-822	1983
	Polydor, POCJ-1895 [Japan]	

"Best of . . .," Selections from "Eyewitness," "Blades," "Casa Loco," and "Evidence," plus three new tracks featuring: Clifford Carter, Bill Evans, Cafe, Neil Jason, and Chris Parker:

"Helping Hand"	Polydor, POCJ-1896 [Japan]	1987

Duet with Rob Mounsey, keyboards, featuring acoustic guitar:

"Local Color"	Denon, 33CY-1840	1987

Steve Khan and Eyewitness recording featuring Anthony Jackson, Dave Weckl, and Manolo Badrena:

"Public Access"	GRP Records, GRD-9599	1989
	Polydor, JOOJ- 20364 [Japan]	

Trio with Ron Carter, acoustic bass, and Al Foster, drums:

"Let's Call This"	Polydor, POCJ-1060 [Japan]	1991
	Bluemoon, R2 79163	1991

Trio with Ron Carter, acoustic bass, Al Foster, drums, and Quartet with Anthony Jackson, bass; Dennis Chambers, drums; Manolo Badrena, percussion:

"Headline"	Polydor, POCJ-1115 [Japan]	1992
	Bluemoon, R2 79179	1992

Steve Khan and Eyewitness recording featuring Anthony Jackson, Dennis Chambers, Manolo Badrena, and Michael Brecker:

"Crossings"	Verve, POCJ-1217 [Japan]	1994
	Verve, 314 523 269-2	1994

Featuring John Patitucci, Jack DeJohnette, Don Alias, Bobby Allende, Marc Quiñones, and Cafe:

"Got My Mental"	Dan Contemporary [Japan]	1997
	Evidence	1997

Publications

Pat Martino Guitar Solos: The Early Years	CPP Belwin
The Wes Montgomery Guitar Folio	Gopam Enterprises
Steve Khan and Eyewitness Songbook/Guitar Workshop Series	Warner Bros. Publications

As Producer

"Two for the Road"	Larry Coryell and Steve Khan	Arista, AB 4156	1977
		BMG B19D-47025	1988
"Step It"	Bill Connors	Evidence ECD 22080-2	1985
"Inferno"	Bireli Lagrene	Blue Note, CDP-7-48016-2	1987
"Foreign Affairs"	Bireli Lagrene	Blue Note, CDP-7-90967-2	1988
"Time In Place"	Mike Stern	Atlantic, 7-81840-2	1988
"Jigsaw"	Mike Stern	Atlantic, 7-82027-2	1989
"Fantasia"	Eliane Elias	Blue Note, CDP 7-96146-2	1992
"Paulistana"	Eliane Elias	Blue Note, CDP 7-89544-2	1993

Original Pen and Ink by Jean-Michel Folon. Given to Steve as a gift for a possible songbook cover in 1980.
Actually became an early sketch for a beautiful poster found mostly in Europe.